heart
led
living

heart
led
living

When Hard Work Becomes Heart Work

Sue Dumais

First Published in Canada 2014 by Influence Publishing

Typeset: Greg Salisbury
Author & Cover Photographer: Adrienne Thiessen of Gemini Visuals Creative Photography

To my soul sister and mighty companion Lisa,
for reminding me to keep following my heart no matter what.

Testimonials

"The only path with any sustainable meaning is heart work. In Heart Led Living, Sue Dumais shines her unique light on this path."
Christiane Northrup, M.D., ob/gyn physician and author of the New York Times bestsellers: Women's Bodies, Women's Wisdom, and The Wisdom of Menopause

"Sue Dumais will challenge you to stand in your power, get out of your comfort zone and stand up for what you believe in. Sue's message comes from her heart. It will stop you from running and make you face the truth of who you are, and that will set you free so that you can manifest your greatness."
Les Brown, Speaker, Speech Coach, Author

"Engaging and Enlightening. Simply Brilliant."
Isabelle Mercier, Brand Strategist & Business Performance Catalyst, LeapZone Strategies TV Show Host, LeapTV.com

"So many people aspire to be their own best version of themselves; however, many find difficulty in how to achieve it authentically. Constantly fighting between ego versus spirit, heart-led versus intentional, Sue Dumais' Heart Led Living shows us how miracles can truly happen when our lives are led by our hearts. This book guides us beyond our internal tug-of-war to a place where we listen to our bodies, take our intuition more seriously, so we acquire the ultimate self-care, and it shows how we should never compromise ourselves any longer."
Belynda Lee, Speaker, Author

"Heart Led Living is a transformational guide where Sue Dumais demystifies living from the Ego and provides a framework so the world can now live In-Spirit. She provides powerful tools and strategies to support the reader to Heal, cultivate their Intuition and live a Heart-Led Life."
Sukhi Muker, Award Winning Doctor, Author, Speaker, Ultra Endurance Athlete

"It has been said that: 'Out of the abundance of the heart flow the issues of Life.' Sue Dumais has captured the essence of that Truth, and has made it her own. Whether or not you agree with her conclusions is not nearly as important as keeping an open ear to the things she will share that resonate with 'your heart' and stir your soul. Heart Led Living is not just a book title, but a well-thought-out expose of a woman and her journey to the center of who she was meant to be: a woman who now has an insatiable passion for guiding others to the still small voice within that must no longer be ignored. Let those that have an ear, hear what the Heart is saying to the soul, and follow!"
Dwight Pledger, Speaker, Trainer, Coach

"I have been immersed in Heart Led living and practicing these principles for over a year. Along this journey I have been incorporating them into my daily life and teaching my kids to come from a place of love not fear, which is truly an incredible gift I can give to my children. I am empowered to continue to bring these teachings into my life and my children's life because of the rewards we have all experienced ... miracles do happen, speaking from experience. Sue's book is an amazing tool for me to remember as well as delve deeper into the founding principles of Heart Led Living. I love Sue's stories and anecdotes; they resonate with me and evoke emotions, and I feel like I received a gift each time I pick up the book."
Kimberly Shuttleworth, Health and Wellness Coach, Mompreneur

"*Sue Dumais' book* Heart Led Living *is how I unearthed some of my deepest fears around speaking up, shining too brightly, and doing whatever I could to just fit in to feel loved; in effect, dimming my own light and not wanting to stand out or find success to the point where someone would proclaim 'what does she know anyway?'.*

After embracing the 10 principles in Sue's book, it became crystal-clear why my deepest desire as a Preschool teacher is to have every child leave my classroom full of curiosity and wonder, but more importantly to know without a doubt they are capable, they matter, and their voice matters! The 'ah-ha' moment was discovering that the piece I most wanted to heal in the world was actually the piece I most needed to heal within myself.

By applying each of the 10 heart-led principles, especially the first 'be willing to healing', you will be able to shine light on all the ways you are playing small and living your life from the sidelines. They say that when the student is ready the teacher will appear. I believe that if this book and the 10 heart-led living principles have found their way into your awareness then there is an opportunity for an awakening and deep healing. The world needs you, so what are you waiting for? Miracles await."

Catherine Burnett, Early Childhood Educator, Founder of Early Discoveries Pre-School and Kid's Club, 2006 Prime Minister Award Winner

Acknowledgements

As I take this moment to feel the deep gratitude in my heart I feel honoured to have so many people in my life to thank. I will begin by thanking my Grandmother and Grandfather who taught me the true meaning of unconditional love. I have so many precious memories of the summers at the cottage and the love you both held in your heart for me always.

To my Father, who reminded me that my life is worth living and to never die with my music in me. I welcome your continued visits in my dreams and I am grateful for our continued relationship from beyond this physical realm.

To my Mom, who sacrificed so much as a single mother to provide me, my sister, and my brother with a loving home. I am so grateful for your courage and sheer determination to make a better life for us. You taught me to never give up and that there is always hope.

To my beloved husband Steve; there are few words that can capture the gratitude I have for you. You bring so much love into my life. You give me full permission to be me. Your support and belief in me is unwavering even when you don't understand why I make the choices I make. We have been through so much together and I know it has strengthened the love we have for each other. Thank you for being such a solid foundation of strength and support in my life.

To my children Hayden and Sarah; I thank Spirit every day for my precious family. I am honoured to share these words of wisdom with you and I am grateful to learn so much from both of you. You are my most cherished teachers.

Thank you to my sister in law, Adrienne Thiessen, who provided the beautiful bio and cover photos. Your passion and talent as a photographer are obvious and your desire to capture the memories for families runs deep in your heart.

To all my "Heart Led Living" members, thank you for listening to your heart's YES. Your commitment to heal and awaken your soul warms my heart. I have learned so much from each one of you and I am honoured to be witness to such incredible courage. As we continue to support each other in achieving our highest potential by aligning with our heart's path we create a ripple effect that will be felt in all corners of the globe.

To my speaking coach and mentor, Les Brown, I thank you for seeing the greatness in me when I struggled to see it myself. I have learned so much from you, but the biggest gift that I will forever carry in my heart is your unconditional love and friendship.

To my mentor, Dr Christiane Northrup, thank you for being so brilliantly brave as you paved the way for the others to trust their own inner wisdom. Your courage and divine strength to speak your truth inspires me to do the same.

To my soul sister, mighty companion, heart-led coach and best friend, Rev Lisa Windsor. You have infused so much love into my life that it is difficult to capture in words just how much of an impact you have created. We have spent many lives and many years supporting each other through the darkness back into the light. Thank you for always being there to remind me of the truth in my heart.

To all my mighty companions; as we walk hand in hand, heart to heart, side by side, my life has truly never been richer. I see you! I appreciate you! I love you! From the bottom of my heart, the depth of my soul, thank you thank you thank you!

Heart hugs and so much love ~
Sue

Contents

Foreword

On the spiritual path, it is rare gift to know a person that lives with a total commitment to their own healing. Only those who first have the true experience of being healed can truly extend that miracle to others. I have been blessed to be a first hand witness to Sue Dumais' journey. I have had the blessing of being her friend and soul sister. And now, I am so excited that others, too, can experience a sacred connection with Sue as she shares the personal stories and powerful revelations she has received on her heart-led path.

When Sue told me that she intuitively felt that there was a book that would be written, I knew it was only a matter of time before the words would flow through her heart on to the pages. Trusting the Spirit, she waited with divine trust for the inspired action steps to flow. Sue uses everything that arises in her life as the backdrop for her healing. All situations, relationships, and projects, including this book, are used to remove the blocks to love's awareness. The stories that she weaves through each chapter, combined with the heart work exercises and spiritual wisdom, create a unique experience for the readers to heal the obstacles they are facing in their own lives right now.

This book is a catalyst for true inner change. And it doesn't stop there! Many readers will want to apply these spiritual teachings in their own lives. Sue has created a heart-led living community that brings the ideas in the book to life. Members have first-hand access to calls, meditations and tools that will help integrate the amazing wisdom in this book. Heart-led living is about living the principles, not just talking about them. Expect miracles on this path!

Allow Sue to be an inspiration on your spiritual journey. This book represents a powerful symbol of love and is a gift to the entire planet. Sue is a miracle worker; she has the courage to follow her heart and share her heart-led journey. I extend tremendous gratitude for her willingness to heal herself and share her gifts with the world.

With Love,
Rev. Lisa Windsor

Introduction

I was born in Kitchener, Ontario, Canada in 1971. Although my parents were still together when I was born, they didn't have a healthy relationship. My father was an alcoholic and they argued a lot. I actually have early memories of them fighting and I could feel the anger, hurt, and sadness deep in my heart like thorns. I am the middle child of three: my brother is one year younger and my sister is two years older. When I was two years old, my mother packed us up and left my father in hopes of creating a better life for us.

Being a single mom was not common in 1973. My mother worked hard to provide for us and often had two jobs just to make ends meet. She did her best to hide her stress and worry, but I could feel all her stress and worry deep in my body.

In fact, I soon realized I could feel the emotions of everyone I came in contact with.

As early as I can remember, I would sit in a room and feel the physical pain and emotional turmoil of everyone there. It would enter my body like thorns of stabbing pain, and I grew up believing the world was full of pain and suffering. I thought I was a "freak" and the ability to feel the pain of others deep in my own body was a form of punishment from God. Little did I know this "curse" would one day become my greatest gift.

When I was around five years old, I was sexually-abused by a group of teenagers. It left a scar that would cause me to spiral downward in feelings of self-blame and deep shame. I became desperate to numb the pain, my own and everyone else's. Carrying the pain of the world became too much to bear and I was willing to do anything to find relief. I felt as though I was a burden to this world, especially to my mother. If I had not been born, maybe my parents would have stayed together.

I asked myself the question "Why?" a lot. Why was I here? Why is there so much pain? Why am I being punished? What is my purpose?

Over the years, I did everything I could to numb out the pain. It felt as though I was dying inside, so I started using food as a source of both comfort and punishment. I was trying to feed my soul, because I felt so disconnected from my sense of self. In 1990, I started exercising every day and teaching fitness classes. Yet, I woke up one morning and realized my eating disorder was completely out of control. I went for counselling for my anorexia in 1993 and my journey of self-discovery began.

While my relationship with food improved, my relationship with alcohol was the next vice I adopted in an attempt to numb the pain I felt deep within. Drinking allowed me to let go of control, numb the pain, and finally have some fun. It took me another eight years to face the truth that my relationship with alcohol was out of control. In 2001, I decided to quit drinking for thirty days; I felt empowered by my sheer determination and commitment.

Two weeks later, I discovered I was pregnant and my entire life changed direction. I finally felt a sense of purpose, and the void I had felt in my life was suddenly filled with the warmth of the baby growing inside me and the idea of becoming a mother. Three months later, I had a miscarriage. I was devastated. It was the most painful time in my entire life, physically and emotionally. After crawling out of isolation, I turned all my energy and efforts into getting pregnant again.

2001 and one was my year of awakening through powerful life challenges that inspired deep healing. In August, my father passed away from cirrhosis of the liver. Sitting with him as he took his last breath broke my heart and inspired me to honour his life by changing the course of my own.

I was committed to heal at the deepest possible level. I became uncompromising in healing all burdens and pain from my past, and my relationship with food and alcohol started to shift. I grew to love my body and trust its wisdom. My desire to be a mother was so strong, I knew what I needed to do. I began to mother myself so that I could be a better mother to my future children. I set a clear intention to be open to find the man who was meant to be my husband and the father of my children.

A few weeks later, I met my husband Steve and my heart expanded with the excitement of becoming a wife and a mother. Right away, I knew in my heart he was the one, but I was afraid it was "too good to be true." He patiently encouraged me to release my fears, open my heart, and receive his love. Steve was a single dad with a beautiful three-year-old girl named Sarah. She welcomed me into her life with an open heart. While I was grateful to be her second mom, my heart yearned to experience another pregnancy.

Steve and I decided to start trying to get pregnant. It took a couple of years to conceive our son. It was an intense month-by-month emotional roller coaster. Steve became my rock solid support and our relationship strengthened. Our dream finally came true, and our son Hayden was born in 2004.

A year later, that yearning deep in my heart to have another child grew strong again. We decided to get pregnant again. This time, I wanted the experience to be different with less stress and worry. Yoga had helped me conceive my son, so I decided to start teaching yoga classes on fertility. I was inspired to open Family Passages Mind Body Studio in Vancouver, Canada, and start teaching fertility yoga classes to support myself and other women and couples struggling to conceive. It became the first studio in Canada to specialize in yoga for fertility, fertility support, and pre- and post-natal health and fitness.

Three years later, I started to notice my skin yellowing. It was a condition called jaundice caused by my liver being in stress. I realized another pregnancy would not be healthy for me and was no longer an option. We turned our focus to adoption and began the home-study process to adopt a little girl from Africa.

I have always felt a heart connection to Africa and our path was clear. For three years we wholeheartedly pursued the process of adoption. We slowly moved up the waitlist until one morning in meditation I received the insight from my heart to let go of the idea of having another child. Today, with our daughter Sarah and our son Hayden, our family feels complete, and the yearning deep in my heart transformed into nurturing and supporting others to heal.

Every decision I made after that was from my heart. I started to trust my heart more than my head. As I deepened in listening to my intuitive heart and aligning with my true teacher, Spirit, I learned how to harness my "curse" and embrace my gift as an intuitive healer. The pain I had felt from others as a child became a tool that continues to allow me to help others experience the miracle of healing. My life's purpose became crystal clear: to inspire and empower healing in myself and others. I went from feeling as though I was dying inside to discovering my YES for life!

Everything was flowing beautifully and, in April 2011, I miraculously manifested $500,000 and we moved to a hobby farm just outside Vancouver. We now have a horse, two goats, eight chickens, cats, and dogs; and our daughter has a snake. It was always our dream to own property and have lots of animals. Our dreams were coming into fruition and our financial challenges transformed overnight.

In July, I was guided to close Family Passages Mind Body Studio and focus on my international speaking career. I was excited to teach others how to trust their intuition, lead with their heart, and align with their heart's path. My dream was put on hold when I realized through my intuitive gift that I had cancer in my body. This was the biggest wake-up call of all, and I realized that in order to be of service in this world, I needed to learn how to fill my heart first and give from the overflow. After taking time to heal and establish a ritual of vibrant self-care, I felt a renewed sense of excitement to share my heart's message with the world.

I was inspired to give birth to my *Heart Led Living* community in January 2012. While I had already been leading with my heart for years at that point, teaching others allowed me to deepen into the ten founding principles of *Heart Led Living*.

Heart Led Living is my business; it is this book; even more importantly, it is every moment of my life. With every breath, I use these principles and I am excited to share them all with you. I share the stories of my life to give you real-life examples of how you can apply these tools. Each chapter is based on one of the ten principles and includes "Heart Work" to help you integrate these principles into your life so that "hard work becomes heart work" in your life, too.

The ten founding principles of *Heart Led Living* are

1. Be willing to heal **FEB**
2. Choose love
3. Hold your light
4. Take inspired action only
5. Fill your heart first
6. Be open to anything
7. Be curious
8. Be attached to nothing
9. Lead with your heart
10. Expect miracles

Spirit designed life to awaken our souls. Are you ready to discover how you can be heart-led in every area of your life? Let's begin our journey together; I am honoured to share my life and heart with you.

Chapter 1

Heart Led Living Principle ~ Be Willing to Heal

We are each here to heal with the intention of evolving our souls. We came into this physical world to have the experiences we most need to heal at the deepest possible level. When we embrace this truth fully and completely, life becomes a playground for healing. Every experience becomes an opportunity and our life becomes the backdrop for our healing journeys. It all begins with our willingness to heal and our commitment to awaken our soul. We can do this either by default or on purpose. When we make a conscious choice to heal at the deepest possible level, life's challenges become more manageable and we live with a deep sense of purpose and trust. When we set a clear intention to release and heal anything and everything that is no longer serving us, life provides every opportunity we need to achieve that. As we embark on this journey together, I ask that you open your mind to new perspectives and simply be willing to heal.

Listening to the Whispers

We are all born with a natural ability to heal. Our bodies speak to us constantly. They send us messages and give us signals all the time. They let us know when we are in harmony and alert us when we are in disharmony. The signals often begin as whispers, wanting to get our attention. These occur when the first signs of disharmony appear. When we listen closely we can catch the message as a whisper, which commonly shows up as a little niggling of resistance or pain. If we miss the first message, the body sends a stronger and more obvious signal, and the pain becomes stronger and more intense. If we continue to ignore it, we will eventually get hit by a two-by-four or hit the brick wall. This is when we have no choice but to listen.

In June 2011, I was sitting in meditation in my Mind Body Studio in Vancouver, Canada, seeking some insight and clarity on the direction of my business. It had been six years since I had opened my studio specializing in teaching yoga for fertility, as well as other programs that supported women through conception, pregnancy, and postpartum health. I was very dedicated and passionate about my work. Not only was it therapeutic for my clients, but it also offered so much personal healing for me around my own fertility challenges.

As I sat in silence, open to guidance from my intuitive heart, I heard the words: "It is time to close the studio". I had learned to trust my intuition so deeply that I didn't even question it. As I sat with this fresh idea, I felt a deep sense of relief; a weight lifted off my shoulders. I felt a renewed sense of adventure, thinking of the free time and energy I would have to travel and speak to the world. Within four weeks, I had closed my studio, and I drove away with the warmth of gratitude in my heart and excitement about the launch of my new global speaking career. Little did I know that the Universe had another path in mind, one that would challenge me to the core of my being.

The month after closing my studio, I was exhausted. I didn't realize just how tired I was until I stopped and listened to my body. Apparently, it had been trying to get my attention all this time, but I was just too busy to notice. When I look back at that time, I realize I was terrified to face the truth. I had been having many health issues since my pregnancy and the birth of my son in 2004. I thought I was doing all the right things through diet, yoga, meditation, health care support, and energy healing, but my body was healing very slowly.

There was a piece of the puzzle I was missing.

When I found stillness and took time to tune into my body, I was drawn to my abdomen and pelvic area. These two areas were the loudest in the way of symptoms and upset. As my awareness deepened I opened to receive messages from my body. The word "CANCER" immediately came into my mind. My eyes popped wide open as my entire body shook with fear. There was my brick wall looming right in front of me and it didn't feel good. How had I missed the whispers?

I have since learned that in order to tune into the whispers, I need to create space and time for stillness and awareness. Most people go through their days on fast forward, jumping from one thing to the next. When I was working hard, I was passionate and loving what I was doing, but I worked ten- to twelve-hour days during the week and spent a lot of time on weekends working on my computer or facilitating instructor-training programs and workshops.

Interestingly, I felt as though I had fought so hard to conceive my family, yet I had very little time and energy to spend with them. How was this living? I wasn't thriving; I was surviving. While I did have my own self-care practice in place, it was just enough to keep me afloat. I was in survival mode, like most of society, but because I was doing what I loved to do, I could justify it on some level. While I could convince myself that I had balance, my body certainly didn't reflect that. I no longer strive for balance in my life; instead, I have learned the importance of maintaining a sense of harmony. When your heart, mind, and soul are in harmony, you can consciously operate at a deeper level of awareness. I was doing a lot to take care of myself, but it wasn't enough, because I was missing a few pieces of my health puzzle. I needed to discover and shine light on the root of the disharmony. So I began creating time for deep listening and tuning into every whisper.

Here is one exercise that I practised regularly, as well as took my clients through, to increase awareness around the body's whispers and messages.

Heart Work: Full Body Scan

Find a quiet place to lie down on your back with support around you to ensure comfort. Find stillness and silence by removing all distractions (turn off phones, etc.). Take ten deep breaths, encouraging the lengthening of each inhale and exhale. It is not about forcing your breath; it is about inviting the breath to lengthen, and imagining the muscles of the back, chest, and ribs softening.

After ten breaths, return to a normal breathing pattern and gently scan your body starting from your toes. Ask yourself, "What's happening in my toes?" Be curious and observe without judgment. Next move to your feet and ask the question, "What's happening in my feet?"

Slowly move up the body taking time to check in with each body part. If you discover some tension or resistance in a certain area, ask, "What do I need to learn from this tension or resistance?" Be open to any insights that come. Don't think about the answer. Allow the answer to come into your mind. "What do I need to do to release this tension or resistance?" After you have completed the full body scan, take five deep breaths and open your eyes. Take some time to reflect and journal about what you discovered, and be curious about any further insight that may come.

Awareness is the first key to healing.

I'm Not Normal

Mother Teresa said it so eloquently, "God, I know you only give us what we can handle. Sometimes, I wish you didn't have so much faith in me."

There may be times in life when it seems as though the Universe is throwing challenge after challenge our way. How we handle those times of perceived chaotic clusters will determine our experience of them and will ultimately influence the outcome.

I have come to recognize these clusters as spiritual awakenings. It is as if the Universe is calling on us to heal, expand, and step into something bigger. These clusters of challenges are enough to shake us up, wake us up, and cause us to pay attention.

> These clusters of challenges are enough to shake us up, wake us up, and cause us to pay attention.

Someone said to me once, "When the ground is shaking beneath your feet and you look around to see what could be causing it, sometimes you discover it is the Universe doing the shaking."

Instead of asking, "Why?" and dropping into the victim role, I encourage you to be curious about what you are meant to learn. Every challenge is an opportunity to heal and grow.

In my case, I was being called to embrace the gift that I had been running from most of my life. Let me explain.

When I was a little girl, my uncle nicknamed me "Squeak", because I would rarely talk and I was painfully shy. That was how it appeared from the outside, but it certainly wasn't my reality on the inside. As I sat and observed everyone in the room, I could feel their pain, both emotional and physical pain. I would pick up on their fears, grief, shame, guilt, and sadness, and at the same time I would feel their physical pain in my physical body. If someone was experiencing hip pain, I would feel pain in my hip. If another person had a shoulder injury, I would feel pain in my shoulder. I never understood it. All I knew was that there was a lot of pain in this world and I was carrying it physically and emotionally. It would come on suddenly like thorns constantly pricking me and I had no way of escaping it. For the longest time, I thought I was cursed or being punished. The few times I tried to explain it to someone, I was told never to talk about it. I thought I was abnormal, a freak. I ran from it for a long time because it terrified me. I did everything I could to numb it. It led me to self-destructive behaviour, until one day I realized I wasn't cursed after all.

I had a friend who had experienced chronic pain for years. One day, I was intuitively guided to bring her awareness to the pain, and I was shown visions about what it was related to and where it was rooted. While it was showing up in her physical body as the symptom of pain, it was actually rooted in her emotional body. It was an emotional trauma rooted in her childhood as an experience of deep shame. When I talked to her of this, memories of her childhood flooded in and tears rolled down her cheeks as her body shook uncontrollably. I was guided to hold a sacred space as she expressed this long-held-back energy.

A sacred space is the ability to be a compassionate witness for an individual's healing or emotional expression with non-judgment. It is about holding a space of unconditional love and compassion so that they feel safe and supported.

Once my friend's tears ended and her shaking stopped, she opened her eyes and asked me, "Where did it go?"

"Where did what go?" I asked curiously.

"The pain, it's gone," she said.

I was in awe of the miracle that had happened before my eyes. I felt humbled as I realized that I had actually helped facilitate her healing.

I became excited about helping others heal using my gift. I learned how to control the messages coming to me by practising what I call "minding my own business", especially in public places. I explain this process fully in Chapter Three. Today, I embrace my gift as an intuitive healer. I am able to tune into a client and read their five bodies: their physical, mental, emotional, energetic, and spiritual bodies. I help them identify the root of their disease or symptoms in these different bodies. Many times, a client will have symptoms in their physical body that are actually rooted in their emotional body.

Everyone is familiar with the physical body, but if we go beyond what we can see with our physical eyes, we can tune into the other four bodies. As an intuitive, I often say I help others see the invisible. When I work with someone, I sense and see more than my physical eyes see.

Here is one way I can explain it. I am shown five pieces of a puzzle and each piece represents one of the five bodies: the physical, mental, emotional, energetic, and spiritual bodies. As I tune into each body or puzzle piece, I am shown what needs to heal in each one. I am guided to the root of the problem and I receive messages about what the client needs to know before it can be cleared.

I recently received intuition around a client's husband. I actually saw him having a heart attack and dying. When I spoke to them initially, I didn't share my specific vision but I was guided to communicate to him the importance of taking a leave of absence from his work. I shared with him, "You either leave work for a period of time to reduce stress and take care of your body or something worse will happen." I actually was told to use these words: "You either leave work now or leave this earth."

While that may sound harsh when you are reading it here, it was exactly what he needed to hear to take the steps he needed to take. On a deep level, he already knew that, but it was as if he needed permission or guidance from someone else. His doctor discovered after a few months of being off work that he needed heart bypass surgery. When I tune into his energy now, I no longer see the vision of him having a heart attack. I see a vision of him smiling and enjoying time with his family.

I have helped hundreds of people become aware of root blocks and helped them heal at the deepest possible level. A root block is like a weed with deep roots that represents a past unresolved trauma. When you remove the root block or weed, the expression of that block is cleared and healing is possible. My entire life, I have had a strong desire to help others, so when I fully realized the effects my gift could have, I thought to myself, "This is my chance." The problem was that I was so focused on helping others and giving my time and energy to anyone who was seeking to heal, that I didn't realise it came at a great cost to myself. In the effort to help others, I neglected to help myself.

Health struggles were not new to me, but I always seem to

manage them well enough to get by. Whenever I got medically tested, part of me wanted so badly for the tests to be normal. Probably because I always thought I was abnormal. I spent my entire life hiding the "real me" from others. I lived in fear of my gift, because I was terrified that others would judge me, that they wouldn't like me, or would think I was a freak.

Back to 2011, when I became aware of the possibility of having cancer in my own body. My challenge was to find a doctor with whom I could share my story without him thinking that I needed to see a psychiatrist. "What are they going to think if I walk in and tell them I have cancer?" Not because I have had a test and been diagnosed, but because I just have this deep intuitive knowing that I do. I am sure you can relate to the fear of judgment. We are taught by society to worry and fear what others are going to think of us. It often paralyzes people and stops them from taking action. Even as I write about this experience, I feel a slight twinge of fear. What will others think? In fact, there are very few people in my life who I have shared my cancer experience with. Writing about it in this book is exposing my truth and that can sometimes be scary. But here is the real truth. I need to tell my story for my own healing, as well as for the healing of many others who are hiding their gifts. No more hiding. No more fear. I choose love!

> I need to tell my story for my own healing, as well as for the healing of many others who are hiding their gifts.

I am not one to let fear stop me; not anymore. I have wasted too much time and energy on fear, and my heart's calling is too strong now to let fear hold me back. For years, I would repeat affirmations to help transform my fears and limiting beliefs.

I am often comforted by the words I heard at a live event in Vancouver featuring Dr. Wayne Dyer: "What others think of you is none of your business". Not everyone is going to like me and it's okay.

Can you embrace that new way of thinking? It is not your job to convince everyone to like you or to buy into what you have to say. Your job is to stay true to YOU. I am going to show you how to do just that and it begins with releasing your fears around judgment. You cannot feel judged if you don't fear judgment. When you own your truth and release the need to convince anyone and everyone of your likability, you free yourself and them to have their own opinion. Part of this freeing is giving yourself permission to follow your heart, even when it doesn't make sense to others. Fear is not my boss. Not anymore!

My first response was of fear, when I received the insight that I had cancer in my own body, and that was followed by a few weeks of denial. Eventually though, I began to feel a sense of hope and a deep trust that I could heal this. If I could use my gift to help others, I knew I could use it to help me. I was determined to hold faith that I would heal the cancer in my body, even though I had no idea how. I turned inward for more insight. I gave it all over to the Universe, and trusted that I could handle it and that I would be shown everything I needed exactly when I needed it. All I had to do was follow my heart. While this may sound simple it is not always easy.

♥ Heart Work: Ask "What?" Not "Why?"

The quality of the questions we ask will determine the quality of the answers we receive. When faced with a life challenge, ask "What?" not "Why?" Asking "Why?" immediately aligns us with a victim mindset. When we ask, "Why is this happening to me?" we receive answers in the way of evidence proving why we are victims of our circumstances. Life is not happening to us; it is happening for us.

Life is not happening to us; it is happening for us.

> Life is not happening to us;
> it is happening for us.

Asking "What?" allows us to find meaning and will open our mind to a new perspective. One possible conversation I could have had with myself was this:

"Why do I have cancer when I have done so much to change my life? I eat healthy. I exercise. I don't get it."

Instead, I chose to be open and curious about the life lesson, so my conversations went more like this: "Okay. This experience is on my path for a reason and perhaps I don't understand it right now, but I am open to find its meaning. All I can do is follow my heart and remain curious, one breath at a time, one step at a time. What can I do in this moment to support my body to heal?"

What is My Health Worth to Me?

Take a moment to ask yourself, "What is my health worth to me?" Many people assume their health will always be there. Some people believe they are invincible. Time and time again, I see people extending love and support toward others yet neglecting their own needs and health. This is especially true in the case of women. You deserve to be healthy as much as anyone else. In fact, you deserve to experience vibrant health. We all do! Your health is priceless and I hope you can come to embrace that truth without having to learn that lesson the hard way.

Less than four weeks after I closed my studio in 2011, I attended the USANA Annual Convention in Salt Lake City, Utah. USANA Health Sciences is one of the world's leading companies in health and nutrition. They develop and manufacture the highest-rated supplements, healthy weight-management products, and self-preserving skin care products. I was introduced to USANA's products by Dr. Christiane Northrup, obstetrician/gynecologist physician and author of the *New York Times* bestsellers: *Women's Bodies, Women's Wisdom* and *The Wisdom of Menopause*. The USANA supplements were the first ones I had ever taken that actually felt like they were doing something. I could sense the nourishment reaching deep into my cells. Within eight months of taking the products, many of my health symptoms improved dramatically. After becoming a USANA distributor, I looked forward to the annual convention and I was excited to hear all about the new product announcements. It was also an opportunity see friends and team mates from all around the world, including Dr. Northrup.

Although I was tired, I still felt strong enough to travel. It was a four-day event and I had decided to start one of my days by attending a meditation led by one of the doctors who had come from Sanoviv Medical Institute. Like USANA, Sanoviv was founded by Dr. Myron Wentz; the Institute is located in Rosarito, Baja California, Mexico. Sanoviv is a state-of-the-art facility that offers alternative, holistic, and integrative health programs to treat a wide range of diseases. The morning at USANA's 2011 Annual Convention began with a lesson in energy medicine followed by a guided meditation led by Dr. Lanzagorta. His words and kindness touched my heart so deeply that I was inspired to speak to him after. I gave him a hug and thanked him for the gift. I felt such pure love and kindness emanating from his heart straight into mine.

Later that day, I felt guided to stop and speak to someone from Sanoviv at the information booth they had set up at the convention. I suddenly found myself sharing my health challenges with Chris, one of the administrative staff. He suggested I book a free consultation with one of the physicians. In all my years of talking to medical doctors, this was the first time I actually felt heard and validated. The doctor was compassionate and patient as I told him about my health issues. He listened deeply without judgment as I shared my intuition about cancer. He made me feel that everything I said was important, and that my history, emotions, and symptoms were going to provide pieces of the puzzle that would help identify the disharmony and blocks in my body so that I could heal.

I felt a sense of urgency in his voice when he told me, "Sue, you need to come to our clinic in Mexico and I suggest you come now. Normally, intakes take two weeks; but we can fit you in at the end of this week." His words rang true all through my body like alarm bells. It was a wake-up call and my body was begging for me to answer.

Everything inside me was saying YES! My body was vibrating with anticipation, but my mind was stuck on the time and money it would take. After all, we have medical coverage in Canada. In the Province of British Columbia where I live, we make a small monthly insurance payment to cover us against the cost of all treatments, medical emergencies, and tests.

I told the doctor I needed to speak to my husband and I would get back to him as soon as possible. When I got off the phone with the doctor, the first words that popped into my mind were, "What is your health worth to you?" I had no answer to that question, but I had a sense deep inside that if I didn't go right away, something bad was about to happen. Intuitively, I knew if I didn't follow my heart and take the leap of faith, financially and otherwise, the cancer would overcome me and the local doctors would finally have their diagnosis.

I asked my husband, "What is my health worth to you? Is it worth me spending all this money? Is it worth me going away for two weeks at the beginning of the kids' school year?" I explained the knowing I had deep down inside that if I don't go now something bad was about to happen.

He lovingly told me, "Do what you need to do and we will figure it out." His response warmed my heart and it helped me tune into the truth that I am worthy of the time and money. I deserve to be healthy for me and for my family.

At Sanoviv, I saw my doctor every day. There were many different practitioners all collaborating on my case. I learned more about my health in two weeks than I had in the previous seven years. I felt exhausted and sick the entire time from the treatment and detoxification, but I knew it was all necessary. My intention throughout my stay was to reveal anything and everything that was needed in order to heal. I would repeat to myself: "Reveal to heal. Reveal to heal." These two weeks were about my health and healing, and I was determined to make the most out of everything.

Working with a psychologist, I healed deep resentment and

anger related to some of my childhood trauma, and I received some key pieces of my health puzzle through alternative testing that were very validating. I finally understood why I had certain challenges throughout my life after being diagnosed with a genetic liver disorder. As for the cancer, my doctor was willing to run further tests, but when I tuned into my heart I already knew there was cancer. I didn't need proof. Plus, I felt that if I had more evidence it would be harder to heal because my fear would become stronger.

When I left Sanoviv, my liver felt ten pounds lighter from the detoxification treatment I'd received and I was excited about the progress I had made in just two weeks. I committed to following Sanoviv's three-month cancer-prevention program and I felt like I was finally on the fast track to healing.

When I got home, I thought I would be ready to jump back into my work, but life threw me another challenge. The medications, supplements, and continued detoxification were intense and my body needed a lot of rest throughout each day. I had a moment of panic worrying about how I was going to support my family if I couldn't work. I realized very quickly it was going to be a full time job taking care of myself. This insight was connected to why I was guided to close my studio when I did. It wasn't because I was launching my speaking career. It was because I needed to be at home and create a sacred space for my own healing. Luckily, I had established several sources of residual income, which meant I continued to earn income each week even though I wasn't working. The importance of creating residual income was something I had learned from my mentor Dr. Christiane Northrup three years earlier. It was such a gift to have the financial support while I took the time I needed to heal.

The Gap of Resistance

Resistance is the gap between what the mind thinks and what the heart knows. Have you ever been faced with a decision that you knew deep down inside you needed to make, but your head talked you out of it or convinced you it would be too hard? The longer you waited, the harder it was to take action and the worse you felt. Resistance becomes the key to help us identify whether our mind and heart are in alignment. This gap is designed to be painful and uncomfortable, so that we can return to alignment more quickly. The more we ignore our intuition or guidance, the bigger the gap gets and the greater the pain and suffering we feel. Resistance can show up as physical pain, emotions, worry, fear, doors closing, procrastination, opportunities lost, getting fired, a busy signal when calling someone, a niggling deep inside, uneasiness, health issues, and more. When you know how to process resistance, it becomes your friend, signaling there is something that needs your awareness and attention.

> Resistance is the gap between what the mind thinks and what the heart knows.

When I arrived home in Vancouver, Canada, from Sanoviv in Mexico, I experienced great resistance. I had thought I could jump back into my life and schedule, and all would be great. I had a program to follow and I now knew what I was dealing with; so it should be easy, right? It was the opposite of easy. I would wake up, get my kids ready and off to school, and I would feel exhausted and have to lie down and rest. I was jaundiced all the time and felt sick most of the day. The resistance grew in intensity. The more I tried to do, the worse I felt. My body was telling me to rest, yet in my mind I wanted to jump back into work. My body was forcing me to rest and take the time to heal.

I asked myself, "Why is it so hard to function normally?" Yes. I used "Why?" on purpose here, because I felt like a victim for a few days. I decided to stop and find stillness. I was curious about the resistance I felt around resting. I lay down on the floor and closed my eyes. The song "You can relax now" by spiritual singer Karen Drucker played softly in the background. The moment I heard her words, "You can relax now. Come on and open your eyes. Breathe deeply now. I am with you", emotions and thoughts of unworthiness surfaced and I wept uncontrollably. I curled up in a ball on the floor and cried all the tears I had. For twenty minutes I wept, as waves of unworthiness swept through my entire body. I felt unworthy of taking the time to heal. I felt unworthy of the money I spent for treatment. I felt unworthy of love because deep down inside I believed I was unworthy and unlovable.

Then the tears finally stopped and I opened my eyes. I felt lighter and my mind was calm. I heard the words resonate deep in my heart: "I am worthy. I am worthy. I am worthy." They suddenly felt true to me and I believed them with my entire being. While I taught others about self-love, I had never fully applied it to myself.

Now, I had a kinesthetic experience of it and my heart expanded. I knew I was taking this time to heal myself, and at the same time I knew I was going to be able to help many more people by giving myself permission to walk through this process with self-love and compassion. My desire to live became strong and my commitment to heal deepened as I came to the realization that my life matters. I was determined to do everything possible to return to vibrant health so that I could teach others how to do the same.

> My desire to live became strong and my commitment to heal deepened as I came to the realization that my life matters.

Understanding the Phases of Dis-Ease

My Sanoviv doctor introduced me to the three phases of dis-ease and I found it so helpful in understanding my own health challenges. These three phases comprise a valuable tool to share with others and explain why so many people are struggling to make sense of their health symptoms. If more people can understand that dis-ease just doesn't pop up overnight, then they would be more inspired to make the changes while they can, instead of waiting until they get a diagnosis.

Keep in mind that it is possible to be in more than one phase for different dis-eases. For example, someone may have been diagnosed with Diabetes, which is Phase 3, but be in Phase 2 for cancer.

Phase 1 – Mental:

Dis-ease begins in the mental body as a belief or thought that is not in alignment with the truth in your heart. This leads to resistance that shows up as a whisper, resulting in an emotional response (e.g. through stress, anxiety, worry, fear, depression, irritability). Phase 1 is the mental and emotional phase that requires awareness, curiosity, and openness.

Phase 2 – Symptomatic:

In this phase the resistance gets stronger and begins to show up as physical symptoms. Even though people are experiencing physical challenges, most Western medical tests will come back normal. This is where prevention is the key, but often people ignore these symptoms especially when their health-care providers tell them the tests are normal so there is nothing wrong. Most people are in this phase right now and have no awareness. The millions and millions of people who will be diagnosed next year with heart disease, cancer, and other degenerative diseases are currently in Phase 2 of symptoms. You have two choices. Wait for Phase 3 when you will get a diagnosis; or take charge of your own health now and focus on lifestyle changes that will move you into prevention and healing.

This is the phase I was in. I was actually bordering on the next phase when I went to Sanoviv. Phase 2 requires a willingness and commitment to heal and trust in your intuition to lead you back on your path to vibrant health.

Phase 3 – Functional:

Here is the phase where the doctor can say, "Okay. We found your tumour" or "We have confirmed you have this disease." This is the brick wall or wake-up call. In this phase, you have no choice but to pay attention. While prevention measures are still helpful here, treatment is generally the next recommended step. This phase requires strength and determination to heal. Faith is also important.

While it is possible to be completely free from dis-ease, most people move in and out of Phase 1, depending on their level of awareness around their thoughts and beliefs. And I believe anything can be healed. ANYTHING! I have seen many miracles, including clients healing from cancer and other diseases. If you feel the need to strengthen your faith in your ability to heal, I recommend the book *Mind Over Medicine: Scientific Proof That You Can Heal Yourself* by Lissa Rankin, M.D. (published by Hay House, USA in 2013). It is filled with miraculous stories around our ability to heal, as well as a lot of science and research.

♥ Heart Work: Health Check

What phase do you believe you are in?

What changes can you make that would support you in the phase you believe you are in?

Are you committed to healing?

Are you willing to adopt a new perspective on your ability to heal and be vibrantly healthy?

No One Recipe Heals All

There is no one recipe that fits all when it comes to healing. I appreciate the Eastern medicine approach to dis-ease, because they treat the individual not the dis-ease. Even when five patients have diabetes, they do not receive the same treatment and healing protocol. Each patient is assessed based on their individual symptoms, history, and lifestyle, as well as their emotional well-being. The practitioner gathers the pieces of their health puzzle and designs a unique recipe for their healing. Sanoviv offers this type of integrative approach, which I loved and found extremely effective.

For a long time, I thought if everyone just did yoga or if I could just do energy healing for them, they would be healed. Yes, these are both powerful healing modalities but only if that individual is meant to do them. When I finally embraced my gift as a healer, I wanted to help everyone: anyone and everyone who had anything that needed healing, I wanted to help. I couldn't figure out why some people would experience miraculous healings, while others didn't. Was I not trying hard enough? Was I doing it wrong? Did they not want to heal?

During the time I took to heal my body, I received a lot of insight about my gift as well as about how we actually come to heal on the deepest possible level. As I discovered my own distinct recipe to healing, I realized that we all have our own unique recipe. I listened deeply and my heart led me to experience acupuncture; high quality supplements that work at a deep cellular level; guided meditations; restorative yoga; holistic health practitioners; Sanoviv; my hobby farm and all my animals; nature, especially the ocean; journaling; organic foods; juicing; and gardening. Ingredient by ingredient, my own unique recipe took form as needed with divine timing.

I developed such a deep trust in my intuitive heart that I was free from cancer within four months. I woke up one day and it was gone. I felt lighter and more alive than ever. I discovered there is only one recipe that will work for each of us and that recipe is to follow our heart.

Our body knows what it needs to heal. It wants to return to harmony and synergy. When our body has synergy, it means all systems are working together as a team to manage and recover from any challenges or upsets that arise. If we follow our heart, our intuition will lead us every step of the way. This became the foundation of the *Heart Led Living* community I started in January 2012. The gift that came from healing my cancer led me to create a vibrant community of "heart-led" sisters and brothers who, in collaboration, are strengthening their ability to tune in and trust their intuition. As we commit to healing ourselves, we contribute to healing the planet. Through weekly calls, meditations, yoga, podcasts and videos, members experience miraculous healings and transformational coaching as we all hold a clear intention for healing and aligning with our intuitive hearts. Our membership started out by invitation only and has grown quickly into a global family. If you are curious about *Heart Led Living* ,you can learn more at www.heartledliving.com. I will go into more detail and share more tools on how each of us can awaken our intuitive heart throughout the book. For now, I would love to invite you to practise deep listening and being curious and open to your inner guide.

Through creating my sacred healing space, I discovered the most important part of my recipe that was sure to keep me healthy for life. This is one ingredient I would suggest everyone use in their recipe. As I looked back on my work at my studio, I was curious about what had caused me to burn out. I was practising what most people would refer to as extreme self-care. So why was it not enough to keep me healthy? I realized my deep desire to help others came at the price of sacrificing myself. I started to see old patterns playing out where I would receive a call from a client who wanted to book a session and I had to say no because I wasn't healthy enough to help them. That was really hard for me. I felt guilty denying them access to my gift. I thought I was meant to help everyone, and that saying "No" was wrong, until one day an insight came clearly from my heart: "You are only to help those you are guided to help."

Well, that changed everything. I had to be obedient and follow my intuitive heart when it came to saying "Yes" or "No" to clients. Even if I wanted to help them, I could only say "Yes" if I received "a heart yes". At first, it felt unfair (my victim mindset surfaced again), but then I opened my mind to a new perspective and the next piece of insight that entered would change my life forever: "When I follow my heart, everyone is taken care of, including me".

Including ME!

> When I follow my heart, everyone is
> taken care of, including me.

It was a gentle reminder that my life matters and that I deserve to take time for self-care and soul care. I felt a deep shift in my entire being. I realised that I need to fill my heart first and give from the overflow. In doing so, I never get depleted and I can help others without sacrificing my own health and well-being.

You deserve to be healthy, happy, and vibrant. When you follow your heart's path and listen to your intuitive heart, insights will surface that are for everyone's highest good, including yours. This is true collaboration and co-creation. I give you full permission to take care of YOU starting right now!

Everything you need to discover for your own unique recipe to health is available to you. Creating awareness and being open to following your intuition is key. As you delve deeper into the ten *Heart Led Living* principles you will continue to strengthen your trust and ability to receive guidance. We all have our own internal guide leading us on our path. The best teacher is the one within your heart.

♥ Heart Work:
Discovering Your Recipe to Vibrant Health

What are you guided to do for self-care on a daily basis?

What is something that keeps coming into your awareness that can lead you to vibrant health?

Is there a book or a practitioner you are drawn to, or a particular message that resonates when you hear about it?

What is something you always wanted to try?

Are you willing to heal at the deepest possible level?

Chapter 2

Heart Led Living Principle ~ Choose Love

Many spiritual teachers believe that only love exists and that fear is simply an illusion. I have come to embrace this truth for myself, but it took some time for me to unwind from my conditioned fear. Society teaches us to be afraid. Fear is used to manipulate, control, and hold us captive in our own minds and lives. Choosing fear sends us on a path filled with the experience of pain and suffering.

I recently watched the movie *After Earth* featuring Will Smith. In one scene, Will explains to his son how to be free of fear. He says "Fear is not real. In this world danger is real, but fear is a choice." I love that explanation, because it helps me find a way to articulate the difference between perceived danger resulting in fear and a choice for love.

Imagine two people standing on a platform getting ready to bungee jump off a bridge. The first one is afraid of heights and sees only the risk and dangers of this activity. Meanwhile, the second is adventurous and loves to take risks every day of his life. He is excited and looking forward to the exhilaration of the leap. It is all about perception and how we choose to see the world and experience life.

In every moment, we have two choices. We are either choosing love or choosing fear. Love is the soft voice of our intuition guiding us in each moment. When we choose love, we are making a choice to follow our heart and align with our inner guide. The energy of love is pure, perfect, and powerfully healing. The choice for love is available to everyone. The question is what will you choose?

Who is your Teacher?

I wasn't always able to follow my intuition. In every moment we are listening to one of two teachers: Ego or Spirit. Ego is the voice of fear, doubt, and worry. Spirit represents the voice of love, intuition, and inner guidance. In any moment, you have the choice of aligning with one or the other, never both. Love and fear cannot exist at the same time. It is either one or the other. Most people are controlled by their ego teacher and buy into the voice of fear.

For the longest time, I would listen to the voice of my ego. It was the little devil on my shoulder, whispering in my ear, "You are not good enough. You need to do better than that. No one likes you." At other times, it would yell at me, call me names, and be downright cruel. Many people refer to this as negative self-talk. I look at it as the convincing voice of the ego mind. When I was growing up, my ego was a tyrant. It would say things to me that I would never say to anyone else. There was always a storm of negative and demeaning thoughts coming into my mind; it felt completely out of my control.

In the fall of 1992, I held my breath as I stepped on the scale. As I anxiously looked down at the number, it read ninety-two pounds. I felt a momentary sense of relief when I realized I had lost more weight. The relief dissolved quickly as my ego planted a thought, "I wonder if I can get to ninety." As I look back, I can see clearly that at five feet tall, ninety-two pounds was extremely light. My clothes were barely hanging on my body. I had to use a belt with some extra holes just to keep some of my pants up. I was severely underweight; yet at the time when I looked in the mirror I saw a fat girl who needed to lose more weight.

Have you ever looked into a funhouse mirror and seen a distorted image looking back at you? That is what I saw every time. My ego mind was so convincing that I couldn't see the true image in the mirror. I couldn't see my true beauty. I couldn't even see the frail, boney, underweight girl who was dangerously shrinking in size. All I could hear was the voice of my ego ranting and raving constantly in an attempt to control my mind, beliefs, behaviours, and actions.

Here are just a few examples of what I heard in my mind every day:

"You will never be good enough. I don't even know why you are trying."

"You are pathetic. Look at you. You can't even control what you put in your big fat mouth."

"Everything you eat turns to fat. You'd better not eat today; otherwise you are going to become a big fat cow."

"Here you are again after a night of drinking. You did it again. You loser. You think people like you. They hate you! Just look at their faces. They hate you!"

"You want people to like you? You want others to love you? You don't deserve love. You worthless piece of s@#$."

"If you died right now, no one would even miss you. In fact, they would be better off without you. You were a burden to others from the day you were born. Why don't you just do everyone a favour and end it?"

I later learned that this type of intense internal dialogue was typical for someone living with anorexia or bulimia. I have even had to censor it a bit, but I believe you will get the point. My ego was a virus infecting all my thoughts. There was nothing I did right. I was never good enough for my ego, so therefore I was never good enough for me. In truth, my ego wanted me dead. I was dying on the inside, because I gave all my power to my ego. Most people go their entire life controlled by their ego mind. There is no pleasing the ego, yet we try, and try, and try, and try.

In 1993, after going to counselling for my eating disorder, I finally realized I could regain control of my mind and I began to challenge those negative thoughts. No one else could do it for me. It was up to me. I remember reading that I don't have to believe every thought that comes into my mind. And in fact, most of the thoughts we have each day are not true. I became very committed to observing my thoughts. Awareness is the first key.

It wasn't until years later that I recognized I had two teachers in my mind. I was working on taking my power back from my ego. I didn't realize that I had a choice to align with a different teacher. In the beginning, I understood Spirit as being the voice of love. In each moment we have two choices: love or fear. Remember love represents Spirit and ego is the voice of fear. I started to ask myself, "Am I coming from a place of love or a place of fear?" If I noticed I was acting from a place of fear, I would ask, "What would love do in this situation?" I became wide open to a new perspective. Suddenly, I started to hear this soft, loving voice whispering encouraging thoughts into my ear. It is my true teacher. It is Spirit.

> "You can't control the thoughts that come into your mind but you can control the thoughts you dwell on." Les Brown, Motivational Speaker and my mentor and speaking coach.

I became very present while observing my thoughts and recognized a direct connection between my state of mind and my physical symptoms. When I was listening to the voice of ego my body felt heavy, tight, and resistant. When I chose to listen to the voice of Spirit I felt light, open, and free inside. When I recognized that I could choose between the two teachers in my mind, I became committed and determined to heal. I became uncompromising and my will to live was overwhelmingly intense. I knew it was either align with my Spirit and live or slowly die with my ego. I chose life.

It doesn't matter if your ego is in control some of the time or a lot of the time. It doesn't matter how old you are or how long you have been aligned with ego. It is never too late. In this moment and in every moment, you have the ability to choose your teacher. It begins with present-moment awareness and an uncompromising commitment to heal your mind and align with your true teacher, which is Spirit. It doesn't matter how much your ego has been in charge, you can always choose to tune into Spirit. If I can do it, anyone can! There is no better time to begin than right NOW.

> It is never too late. There is no better time to begin than right NOW.

♥ Heart Work: Love or Fear

When you are faced with a challenging situation or feel pressured to make the right choice, ask yourself the following questions:

Q: Am I coming from a place of love or fear?
Q: What would love do in this situation?
Q: How do I feel physically? Do I feel light, expanded, and relaxed (Spirit) or do I feel tight, heavy, and tense (ego)?

You can use the following affirmation to make it clear you are choosing Spirit. Make sure you are saying the words with conviction, feeling, and certainty.

Affirmation: "My ego is not my boss. I choose to listen to the voice of Spirit (or love)."

Healing Process: "I give this situation over to you, Spirit, and I ask for healing. Please heal it on the deepest level. Please show me a new perspective. I am willing to see this challenge through the eyes of love."

Sneaky Gremlins

When we are shifting from ego to alignment with Spirit, our ego will become desperate. We will start to experience what I refer to as ego temper tantrums. We may have moments of feeling wildly out of control like a two-year-old trying to get her way. The ego may get louder and louder, forcing us to pay attention. The ego's survival depends on us buying into the poisonous lies and the fears it pours into our mind. When we learn to manage the temper tantrums and become witness to them, the ego becomes a very sneaky gremlin.

My ego went from being loud and obnoxious, to being sneaky and clever. I would be feeling good and moving in the direction my heart was leading me when suddenly I would hear, "You're an idiot!" I would stop and literally look around and question where the voice came from. When I couldn't figure it out, I would continue on with what I was doing. I eventually realized it was my ego. When I tuned in and asked Spirit for greater clarity, the image I was shown was a sneaky little gremlin hiding behind a tree, peaking out and shouting negative things at me and tucking back behind the tree so I wouldn't see him. Well the moment I became aware of that trick, the gig was up.

It seems every time we get wise to the tricks of our gremlin, he becomes even more of a trickster. When I was guided to let go of my administrative assistant, I was having a difficult time. So I spoke to my husband looking for some words of support. I was explaining that I would go in the next morning and tell her the news, and give her two weeks' severance pay. When I told him that I would then ask her to pack up her stuff and leave, his response was intense, "Well, that's heartless!"

Ouch! That pierced my heart. Instead of getting upset and angry, I remained curious, because it was so unlike my husband to respond that way.

As I went into stillness and opened my mind to insight, I realized that his words were actually a reflection of what I already felt deep inside. I didn't want to fire her, but I knew in my heart I was freeing her and honouring what I needed to do for my business. On some level, I felt guilty and heartless. I thanked my ego for bringing that into my awareness and I processed it, so I could go in the next day with a clear heart and speak from a place of love, without guilt or shame. If I hadn't been practising this level of awareness and curiosity I surely would have gotten angry at my husband and felt unsupported by him. I am grateful I was able to recognize that this reaction was my ego desperately playing tricks to pull me out of alignment with my heart's path.

Our ego thought system is something we create, so we actually have more control over it than we think. The key is to be willing to practise present-moment awareness, and to be curious about any resistance or triggers we feel. At one point, I wanted to condemn my ego. Ban it all together. Eventually I recognized that on some level my ego served me, protected me, and kept me safe. Although it was an illusion of safety, I felt comforted by this strong dominant voice within. It gave me strength in times of fear and at the same time it paralyzed me with fear. It kept me safe by convincing me to play small and not take too many risks. My ego convinced me not to put myself out there, otherwise I might get hurt. But there comes a time when it no longer served me to play safe. I want to take risks now and live life fully. I want to go where my heart leads me, even if it doesn't make sense in my head.

One day in meditation, I actually thanked my ego for everything I had learned and gained from aligning with him as my teacher for so long. I had learned a lot the hard way, but I had learned a lot. I wouldn't be the person I am today without those powerful life lessons. Apparently my ego didn't like that at all, as I saw him march off with his feet stomping in defeat, which made me smile even more.

♥ Heart Work: The Gift of Practising Hindsight

Find stillness and silence, and reflect back on your past experiences. Often, one experience is in your awareness more than another. Go with whatever comes first. Often the guilt or regret we carry from our past is from a situation in which we chose to align with ego. Instead of judging it as good or bad, take a moment to reflect back and find one gem, lesson, or gift that came from it. When you find the gem, you can release the history anchor that

keeps you stuck. Bring the treasure into the present moment and
release the rest. Sometimes we have to forgive to release the history anchor fully. I discuss how to do that in Chapter Four. Your
ego wants you to hold on to past regret, doubts, shame, and fear.
Ego has more power over you when you carry the past with you.
Let go of your past, but bring the gems and lessons with you.
You not only free yourself by doing this, you remove all points
of weakness whereby your ego can pull you into a wormhole
and out of alignment. Remember, we don't heal the past in the
past; we heal how we feel about the past in the present moment.
Healing is occurring now.

We don't heal the past in the past; we heal how we feel about
the past in the present moment.

> We don't heal the past in the past; we heal how we
> feel about the past in the present moment.

Here is an example for you. When I look back at all the unhealthy relationships I had, I used to feel guilt and shame. I
would often blame myself for how they turned out. When I look
through the lens of healing, I see how they all prepared me for
the relationship I have with my husband today. After more than
twelve years together, we never fight, we respect each other's
opinions, and we have a deep love and trust in each other. He is
my rock solid support and he encourages me to follow my heart,
even when he doesn't understand. I have so much more gratitude
and appreciation for my relationship. Part of me wants to say I
am just lucky, but really I can take full credit for being open to
such an incredible man in my life. I am not lucky; I am deeply
grateful that I was able to heal my past, break my self-destructive
relationship cycles, and be open to a new way of being in part-
nership. My past relationships helped me get crystal clear about
what I don't want and what I do want in a relationship, and that
is what showed up with divine timing. My ego tried hard to scare
me away from my husband when we first met, convincing me
it was too good to be true. But my husband was persistent and

followed his heart. Every time I was about to turn and run the other way, he said exactly what I needed to hear to keep me in alignment with what I knew deep in my heart. We are meant to be together, grow together, and love each other deeply. Love trumped ego once again, because I was willing to stay present and break out of my patterns of fear.

Two Kinds of "Feel Good"

When we choose ego as our teacher, everything feels hard, heavy, and we experience a lot of resistance and obstacles. Things don't go smoothly and there are always unexpected challenges that throw us for a loop. When we are in alignment with Spirit, it feels good and everything flows easily and effortlessly. People and support seem to show up exactly when needed, resources align without effort, and we feel like the Universe is working with us.

In *Heart Led Living*, our tagline is "When hard work becomes HEART work." Life is not meant to be so hard and I assure you, life is not out to get you. Life is meant to be joyful, pleasurable, and expansive. When we are in alignment, it feels good to be alive. Life is an exciting adventure. Even in times of sadness, grief, or other lower vibrating emotions, we can still experience a sense of peace, if we don't judge, fear, or deny those emotions. When these emotions show up, simply allow them to express themselves, so you can let them wash through you and release them with love. I promise if you give yourself space to experience them, you will return to your natural state of feeling good and at peace.

> *Heart Led Living: When hard work becomes*
> *HEART work.*

Now I need you to understand that there are two kinds of "feel good." There is the genuine "heart-expanding feel good" when we are in alignment with Spirit. Then there is the "artificial feel good" created by the ego as a way to deceive us and keep us thinking we are in alignment when we are not. Confused yet? That is what your ego wants right now so that you don't understand and embrace this concept. I am exposing one of the tricks of the ego and you may feel some resistance here, so bear with me.

I have always been a student in my life. I am a sponge for new knowledge. I love reading books, going to workshops and seminars, learning new skills, and acquiring new tools. One would think this is a good quality to have. We may assume that people who are open to personal and professional development must be in alignment, but that is not always the case. There was a period of time when I was so busy learning the next new thing, that I barely had time to integrate what I had just learned. I would go from one workshop to the next, to the next, and I thoroughly enjoyed every one of them, but something was not quite in alignment. Underlying my desire to learn was the true motivating factor in my decision to jump from book to book, workshop to workshop, course to course: it was the deep-seated belief that "I am not good enough". My desire to learn more was in alignment with Spirit, but my need to constantly learn was coming from the ego and it was feeding my fears that I didn't know enough, that I wasn't smart enough, that I wasn't qualified enough.

I had known about my old belief "I am not good enough" for many years now, but I only became aware of the two kinds of "feel good" in 2012. I heard about a workshop that promised to be the answer to the challenges I was facing in authentically selling my products and services. I became excited and felt really good about investing over $5,000 to attend the workshop in San Diego. When I arrived home, I reviewed the material and definitely learned a lot, but something didn't feel so good and I just couldn't put my finger on it. One month later, along came another opportunity to learn to market my services and my business authentically and to effectively monetize my message. Everything inside me jumped and I felt this rush of excitement and anticipation. This time, I reached out to talk to my heart-led sister and dearest friend Lisa. She felt my excitement and it sounded good to her, but she became aware of a slight niggling that something was not in alignment.

In *Heart Led Living*, we join with each other and intuitively tune in to decisions or challenges we are facing. This helps with the process of discernment, which I will address in greater detail shortly. I joined with Lisa on the issue of taking the workshop, and instead of focusing on how good it felt to think about going, I tuned into the niggling Lisa was sensing. I felt it deep in my solar plexus, which is where I keep my awareness, and there it grew in size and became more and more obvious to me. The words "You know everything you need to know" came to Lisa. Those words resonated deep in my heart as my truth. The underlying reason why I wanted to sign up for this program was another layer of feeling "not good enough as I was." My ego had learned to disguise itself as an "artificial feel good." For weeks, I explored this idea for myself and with my clients, and I tapped into my ability to help myself and others feel and discern the difference between the two kinds of "feel good."

♥ Heart Work: Feeling Your Heart's "Yes"

Here is a process that will help you identify if you are in alignment with Spirit or are being tricked by your ego:

Find stillness and silence, and take eight deep breaths to centre yourself. Imagine that you can look over to the right side of your mind. Take a few breaths. Now imagine dropping down into your heart space. Set an intention to be wildly open to hear, see, know, and feel.

Imagine yourself standing at a fork in the road. Bring into your awareness the decision you need clarity around and imagine walking down one path that would lead you toward it. Ask a "Yes" or "No" question. For example, "Am I meant to attend this workshop?" or "Am I meant to take this path at this time?" Notice how your body feels. The body holds your true answer.

Tune into the physical sensations particularly around your heart. Do you feel light, expansive, or open? Do you feel heavy, tight, or closed? Do you feel a rush of excitement or a peaceful "Yes"? Is there a part of you that desperately wants a "Yes"?

Now imagine walking down the other path. This path leads to the opposite of your question. Tune in again and notice how you feel physically.

If you felt light, expanded, or open when moving toward a "Yes," that is a heart YES.

If you felt heavy, tight, or closed when moving toward a "Yes," that is a heart NO.

If you felt a rush of excitement and anticipation, almost like an addict getting her next hit, or if you felt desperate for the answer to be "Yes," then that is likely an "artificial feel good" or "ego yes." That translates to a "heart no."

If you completed this exercise and you are still unsure, then wait for clarity or join with another heart-led individual and together you can tune into the "Yes" or "No." We do this all the time during our *Heart Led Living* member calls. Every week, members can bring to the live call a decision they are facing, and ask for support. Together, we can all tune in and help them receive clarity from the heart. The process of all of us joining together can help the person who is making a decision become aware of any niggling or subtle resistance. Discernment is one of the trickiest exercises. I am grateful my intuitive gift has become stronger around this process and that I am able to feel into it for others, helping them discern the difference between a "true heart yes" and an "artificial ego yes." If it is not an absolute heart YES, then it's a NO. If you don't have clarity, wait for it. Keep practising and your intuition will get stronger about this as well.

Big Shiny Carrots

As we start to feel our "true heart yes", the ego starts attempting to derail us with the temptation of "big shiny carrots". Just when we start feeling confident that we can discern our "true heart yes", and we have clarity that we are on our heart's path, the ego dangles a big shiny carrot in front of us. Oh and it is a juicy temptation filled with all the promises we can imagine. While it feels good and exciting, it is the ego's attempt to keep us from following our heart's path. Remember, the ego's supremacy depends on your buying into its lies and deceits. Without your belief in the ego, it will eventually lose power over your mind.

The challenge with big shiny carrots is that we take one step closer and the carrot moves one step farther. For the longest time, I was always just one step away from success or financial freedom. It seemed to be always just around the corner. My ego would come in with some new workshop I could take that promised a huge return on investment, or some job opportunity that promised to fulfill all my dreams. My ego had me always seeking, looking, wanting, and yearning, while everything I wanted deep in my heart was right in front of me.

My ego kept me from financial success, even when it seemed to be speaking in a positive language. I would always say, "I can feel it coming. It is just around the corner. It is so close, I can taste it. I am ready." The problem was that it continued to be just around the corner. I would launch a new program and think this is it. Nope. Okay. Perhaps this one. Nope, not that one either. I kept going, and going, and going, because I kept seeing the carrots dangling in front of me. It was like a dog trying to catch his own tail, which I find hilarious to watch, by the way. It is even more funny now that I realize that is what I was doing, chasing my tail, running after the next big shiny carrot. I was always getting ready to get ready to receive, but not getting to where I wanted to be.

♥ Heart Work: I Am....

"I am" is one of the most powerful statements you can use to manifest. It is a bold affirmation and statement of ownership. Choose your words wisely. For example, if you change your language from "I am ready" to "I am willing," you will go from always being ready into inspired action. When used properly, "I am" is a statement of worthiness, willingness, and openness. Even if your goals haven't yet come into fruition, repeat the statements as if they are already true in your life. Watch for the sneaky ego to come in and use the language of love itself.

> Change your language from "I am ready" to "I am willing,"
> When used properly, "I am" is a statement of worthiness,
> willingness, and openness.

Here are some examples to help you practise a deep level of awareness around your language.

Ego: "I am ready to receive abundance."

Spirit: "I am willing to receive abundance now. I am an abundant being."

Ego: "I am ready to heal and be healthy."

Spirit "I am willing to heal. I am vibrantly healthy."

Ego: "The life of my dreams is just around the corner."

Spirit: "All my dreams are inside me and I choose to say YES to all of them. I am wildly open to receive them now."

Ego: "I am ready to open my heart to receive all that is meant to come to me."

Spirit: "I am wildly open to receive all that is here now and all that is meant to come to me."

Create at least two "I am" statements that are aligned with Spirit right now.

_____

_____

Say them repeatedly throughout the day with power and conviction. Repeat them while looking in the mirror. Look deep into your eyes. The eyes are the windows of the soul. If on some level you don't believe these statements, you will feel resistance.

Observe the resistance without judgment, then ask for healing. Here is an example of what you can say:

> *"I am worthy. I am worthy. I am worthy. I ask that any and all that is not in alignment with this truth be brought to the surface for healing. I choose to heal it at the deepest possible level and embrace this new truth fully and completely. Thank you! Thank you! Thank you!"*

My Ego High-Jacked My Spirituality

This is where we delve deeper into the desperate tricks of the ego. Just when we think we have it all figured out and we believe we are in full alignment with Spirit, our ego high-jacks our spirituality. In a desperate attempt to once more regain control of our mind, the ego begins to use our spiritual practice against us. It figures out how to disguise itself as love. It starts to sound loving, compassionate, and convincing. It uses the language of love and spirituality against us and it feels good on most levels. We believe we are on track, but deep down inside there will be a slight niggling that something is not quite in alignment. This is when it is the trickiest to discern between ego and Spirit. This is when "joining" with other heart-led members can help. "Joining" is a process of tuning in to one another's intuition and guidance. We use our own intuition to discover insight and answers for others. We can often pick up on things that the individual is blind to see or resistant to know. When I am speaking to individuals, or watching them, or reading their materials, I can pick up on the misalignment. It shows up in my awareness and I can see where it is rooted.

I was really hesitant to write about this piece, because my ego was trying to convince me that I was bragging and trying to prove I am better than other people. Who am I to say what is in alignment for another person? Who am I to say whether other Spiritual teachers aren't in full alignment? Who am I to judge that they are operating from their ego, without their awareness, in spite of their spiritual practice and teachings? Does that make me better than them?

My answer to my ego is, no, not at all! I am doing my heart work every moment of every day, and I know my ego is still finding its way in. I am not in perfect alignment all the time. It is not about judging that others are doing it wrong, or about pointing out that they believe they are walking their talk when they are actually not. When you remove judgment and become neutral, you begin to observe and be witness.

> When you remove judgment and become neutral, you begin to observe and be witness.

It took me quite a while before I even began to speak about this awareness, because I was afraid of how others would take it. My intuitive gift is to help others feel the intangible so they can be in true alignment with Spirit and expose how their ego is disguising itself as love. It is a gift I am inspired to share in spite of the ego fears that arise.

When I first heard Debbie Ford was struggling with cancer it was about a month before she passed away. Debbie was an author, healer, and spiritual teacher. Her spiritual work was teaching about the Shadow Effect. Her work has helped many heal their deepest, darkest secrets, and free themselves from their past. I was listening to an interview she had with Oprah in which she was sharing about her battle with cancer. After ten years, she had finally opened up about it. She was in complete denial that she even had cancer for many years, and even when she finally faced the truth, she didn't comment about it publicly. She taught others how to face, expose, and heal their shadows, yet she was holding onto a huge shadow herself, and it was eating her up inside without her awareness. She was in complete denial of it and didn't want to face it. This is just one example of how even spiritual teachers are susceptible to the ego's clever disguise.

When I see others, visit their websites, or just bring them into my awareness, I get a sense of whether they are in full alignment with Spirit or not. I can tangibly feel whether there is even a tiny niggling of ego in their words, body, or energy field. I have come to embrace my gift of discernment, because I have been able to help many people expose their ego. Even with my level of awareness, I am not immune to this ploy of the ego. As I type these words, my ego wants to convince me not to share this because I may offend people (this is an example of ego disguised as kindness). My gift is meant to be shared. I choose to embrace it and use it for the good of all. If I am guided to share with someone about how their ego might have high-jacked their spirituality and I offend them, then that is in some way purposeful. It is not up to me how it unfolds. I choose to be obedient in sharing when I am guided to do so. I follow Spirit no matter what, because I know when I do, it is for everyone's highest good, including mine. Even though someone may get offended, perhaps having that conversation with them could plant the seed of awareness, which later sparks a shift that allows them to align. As long as I am in alignment and follow my intuition, I know my role is purposeful.

♥ Heart Work: Exposing the Ego

As I mentioned earlier, it is tricky to expose ego on our own, especially in the beginning. That is why in our live *Heart Led Living* member calls, we join with one another and practise the tool of discernment. I love when we tune into one member's challenge and we all get similar guidance for them.

Here is a tool you can practise on your own:

Find stillness and silence, and take eight deep breaths.
Bring into your awareness your spiritual practice, teaching, blog, video, message, or whatever you wish to practise discernment around.
Set your intention to align fully with Spirit and be wildly open to any insight or guidance around it. This is the practice of another Heart Led Living guiding principle: "Be attached to nothing."

Repeat the words, "I am willing to see the truth and expose anything that is not in full alignment with Spirit. Please show me if my ego is disguising itself in any way in an attempt to keep me from being a clear and perfect channel for my soul's purpose or message." You can tweak this slightly so it resonates deep in your heart.

Be open. Remain curious. Scan your body and sense any areas that are tight, tense, blocked, guarded, hiding, or niggling. This may take some time, especially if the ego is well hidden. Declare "Reveal to heal!" and continue to gently scan each of the five bodies one at a time in the following order: the physical, mental, emotional, energy, and spiritual body.

If you become aware of any resistance or tension give it over to Spirit and ask for healing on the deepest possible level. Release it with love and gratitude. Remain in stillness until the release feels complete. Then trust that it is healed.

Chapter 3

Heart Led Living Principle ~ Hold Your Light

Imagine how different the world would be if we all had the courage to own who we are. I am sure there are people in your life you can think of right now who seem solid in their message and confident in who they are. If we all had permission to be a full expression of self, the world would instantly heal. We would all stand strong and have the courage to speak our truth. We would all shine bright and share our unique gifts and talents with the world. We would all hold our own light with unshakeable confidence on a solid foundation of love. When we learn to hold our light nothing can dim our love. When we meet fear with love, fear dissolves and our light becomes even brighter. It is time for each of us to hold our light and be a lighthouse of love. Are you willing to stop hiding and start shining brightly once again?

Hide and Seek

Complete this sentence: "If you knew the real me you would..."

So many people are afraid to let others know who they really are. Many of my clients have confessed they have an underlying fear that others won't like them. As a society, we are taught to live in fear. We are afraid to be judged by others. We are afraid of speaking our truth. We are afraid to share our gifts. We are taught even to be afraid of fear itself. We are hiding our true expression of self, yet we yearn to be a full expression of self. We are trapped in an internal tug of war, and fear is holding us captive. Many people walk around wearing masks pretending to be someone or something they are not.

> We are hiding from others because we are afraid, but what is even more painful is that we are hiding from our true self.

"If you knew the real me you wouldn't like me. You would think I was weak, ugly, and deserved to be punished."

That was my internal subconscious dialogue growing up. Ever since I could remember I didn't like myself and I thought if others found out who I really was, they wouldn't like me either. I became a people pleaser, a peace keeper, and I tried my hardest to be the good little girl. It was as if I was living a double life. On the outside, it looked one way, but on the inside, it was a nightmare led by my ego. I grew to hate everything about myself.

I was determined to prove to others that I was good enough. In the eyes of society, I appeared successful. I did well at school and received honours and several awards in college. I was a hard worker from the outside, but a workaholic on the inside. It appeared that I always had money, but I lived with very little money in the bank, because I felt I didn't deserve abundance. I was desperate to keep my secret and convince others that I had it all together. I was teaching fitness classes and educating others on nutrition, while hiding my anorexia. I was working full time holding three jobs when my relationship with alcohol and substance abuse was at its worse. I opened my studio, bought my own loft space, wrote two books (*A Strong Core for Life*, published by Trafford Publishing in 2007 and *Yoga for Fertility Handbook*, published by Trafford Publishing in 2009), ran several of my own businesses, and from the outside seemed extremely successful, yet I felt I was dying on the inside because I felt I was a failure. I spent most of my life running and hiding on the inside, yet appeared to be thriving on the outside. Nothing was ever good enough, because my deep-seated belief was that "I wasn't good enough."

Are you willing to turn your awareness inward and discover the truth about your internal environment? Are you ready to discover who you really are, so you can shine your light bright in this world, without fear?

When we bring awareness and shine light on our internal pain, fears, and worries, we can heal them once and for all. The problem is most of us are afraid to look directly at fear. Our ego convinces us that facing our fear is painful and will accomplish nothing but produce more fear. I promise that if you face your fear and look directly at it, you will find peace on the other side.

♥ Heart Work: The FEAR Process

This is a *Heart Led Living* process to help you process fear. It uses the letters of the word "fear" so it's easy to remember.

Step 1 ~ F – Full-Stop:

The moment you become aware of feeling upset, you can choose to take a full stop. This means stopping all distractions and looking directly at it. Be open and curious. Remember you are never upset for the reason you think.

> Remember you are never upset
> for the reason you think.

Step 2 ~ E – Emptying:

Take a breath and get present to the sense of upset. You may notice physical sensations, thoughts, confusion, worry, anger, or other emotions. Create some space to allow everything that is no longer serving you to come up and empty out from you. Allow the emotion or energy to express itself in whatever way it needs. You may experience shaking, crying, laughter, pain or discomfort, energy shifting or moving, or you may experience nothing. Set the intention to release everything into the arms of Spirit, and give it over for healing.

Step 3 ~ A – Acceptance:

"It is what it is and it's okay." Have no judgment about what is coming up and out. Simply observe, accept, and allow it to be released and healed. Trust that it is being held by Spirit and that healing is occurring. You don't need to understand. You only need to be willing to give it all away to Spirit and let it wash through you.

Step 4 ~ R – Receive:

Be open and willing to receive the healing energy. Be curious about the life lesson or gem that may come into your awareness. You are not actively seeking or looking for anything here; you are simply open to receive with your whole heart. Take a moment of gratitude: "Thank you, thank you, thank you …."

I Am Done Running

Have you ever had an experience of running from something? Did you ever feel afraid, but have no idea why? Do you have a fear of the unknown?

Our ego wants us to be afraid. It convinces us that the world is a scary place and we need to keep ourselves safe from danger. Obviously, this is all reinforced by society, especially the news. In keeping ourselves safe we actually end up playing small, and we become afraid to take risks. Our ego even convinces us to be afraid of fear itself.

I remember having a recurring nightmare as a child in which I was running down a hallway of an apartment building in our neighborhood, and someone was chasing me. I would run to the end of the hallway, down the stairs, and down the next hallway, hoping to gain some distance between us. The fear was intense and all I could do was run. I was running for my life. As I reached the ground floor I could see the exit sign at the end, and I gathered all my strength and courage and ran as fast as I could. If I could just get through those doors, I would be safe. As I reached the end of the hall, I had a moment of relief thinking I had got away. But when I opened the door, there they were. I woke up in a panic, struggling to catch my breath. I knew I had been caught, but I never saw who I was running from. It was always the same dream. It always ended the same way.

Several years ago, I was receiving a yoga therapy session in which I suddenly felt the same deep fear and the need to run for my life. The therapist encouraged me to imagine myself running. I took a deep breath, gathered my courage, and was about to run. But everything inside me said, "No, not this time. I am done running. I have run my whole life. I want to face it." As I imagined myself turning around to face my biggest fear, I started laughing. The therapist asked, "Why are you laughing?" There was nothing there. I was running from nothing. Then I realized that all this time, I was running from myself. I was afraid of my power, my gift, my energy, my potential, I was afraid of myself. I had been running from the gift I am meant to share with the world. Essentially, I was running from my truth.

My ego did not want me to embrace my gift as an intuitive healer and it played every trick it knew to keep me in fear. I would still be running to this day if I hadn't had the courage to turn and face my fear. I have since walked many clients through their fear and every single time, there is light and peace on the other side. Sometimes we need to walk hand in hand with another witness for support. I promise that when you can tap into the divine courage within you and walk through your fear, it is not as scary as you imagined it would be and there is always light and relief on the other side. You can do this! I have complete faith in you!

I have learned so much from my mentor and speaking coach, Les Brown. He is one of the top five motivational speakers in the world and he came into my life at a time when I needed to embrace my calling to speak to the world. I am honoured to be one of Les Brown's Premier Platinum Speakers and I am grateful for his coaching and our friendship. Les Brown always says, "Ask for help, not because you are weak, but because you want to remain strong." If you need support walking through your fear, reach out and ask for help. There are angels all around you ready to support you. Follow your heart and you will be led directly to them.

If you need support walking through your fear, reach out and ask for help.

♥ Heart Work: Cleansing Breath

The energy of fear can be paralyzing and intense, but there is a way to transform fear by using a simple tool like breath work. Psychotherapist Fritz Perls taught that "fear is excitement without the breath". The energy of fear is the same as the energy of excitement. The only difference is that with fear you will be holding your breath, or it will be shallow and rapid. This exercise will help you shift it immediately.

- Find stillness and silence, and bring your awareness to your breath.
- Begin by observing each inhale and exhale. Notice the rhythm of your breath. Be aware of the length of each inhale and exhale. Without judgment, simply observe your breath.
- Invite a longer exhale, creating space for a longer inhale. Imagine fear leaving with your breath out and invite excitement and anticipation to enter with your breath in. Continue exhaling fear and inhaling excitement until you feel the shift.
- Imagine your heart smiling with gratitude and appreciation.

This Is Who I Am

> "I was once afraid of people saying, 'Who does she think she is?' Now I have the courage to stand and say, 'This is who I am.'" Oprah Winfrey, media proprietor, talk show host, and philanthropist.

Truth and honesty go hand in hand. Honesty is about leading with your heart, living with integrity, and owning your truth. It is about having the courage to stand up and say, "This is who I am." For most of my life, I was afraid to be me. I was terrified to share my truth. I was afraid of judgment from others. I was afraid that if they knew the real me, they wouldn't like me. While I wasn't being honest with others, what was even more painful was I wasn't being honest with myself.

We all wear different hats and play different roles in our lives. I am a mother, wife, speaker, yoga instructor, coach, friend, sister—but who am I really? Who are you really? If you remove all the labels accumulated over time, who are you at the core?

You are truth. You are love. Reflect on the extent to which you can stand and declare, "This is who I am." We all have a source of divine courage within us. You have a choice, and you can choose to live from a place of fear or you can own your truth. When in fear, you focus on being who others want you to be or what you believe you should be. As a child, I wanted to be anyone else but myself and I never thought I was good enough. Then there is truth. Our truth is in our heart. It is an expression of our purpose and why we are here on this earth. We need to get out of our heads and into our hearts. We need to be honest with ourselves and trust our own intuition.

The good news is that each one of us has an internal GPS (global positioning system), which lights our path. It is a place within that knows without thinking. Have you ever experienced a moment where you just knew what you needed to do? Today, I trust and follow my intuition even when it doesn't make sense in my head, and especially when it doesn't make sense to others. That means that sometimes you need to stand alone. It takes courage! We can let fear stop us in our tracks but here is the truth: follow your heart no matter what, because the thing you are most afraid of will have the greatest impact on your life and the lives of everyone around you. I promise you, it is so worth it!

> Follow your heart no matter what, because the thing you are most afraid of will have the greatest impact on your life and the lives of everyone around you

Globally we are at a point when running from our truth is no longer an option. It has become far too painful. We have reached a tipping point and there is a shift toward global healing. Even the Earth is calling upon us to awaken to our full potential. Will you answer the call now? Or are you going to wait until you hit the brick wall? The time to heal is now! The time to wake up is now! The time for you to embrace your gift and share it with the world is NOW!

It is time to shine your light brightly in this world. Yes, it takes courage, but you now know that there is an unlimited source of divine courage within you. You owe it to those people that your light is meant to touch. You owe it to the world to share the gift that has been given to you. And most importantly you owe it to yourself to live with integrity and own your truth. The world is waiting for you and we need you now more than ever. It is time to stand in your power, to trust your intuition, and to own your TRUTH.

♥ Heart Work: Soul Declaration

Clear your mind and let go of everything you think you know about yourself. Be wide open and attached to nothing.

- I encourage you to stand up and declare inside your heart and mind, "This is who I am!" Repeat it eight times.

- Do this exercise in front of the mirror, looking deep into your eyes, and set an intention to connect with your Soul. The eyes are a pathway to the soul. Repeat eight times with feeling and conviction, "This is who I am!"
- It is common to feel emotional during this exercise. Create some space to express any and all emotions that arise. Better out than in.

Minding My Own Business

"Be who you are and say what you feel, because those who mind don't matter, and those who matter don't mind." Dr. Seuss, author and cartoonist

Many people I speak to express how they feel sensitive to their environment as well as to other people's energy and emotions. With the global shifts that are occurring, I believe these sensitivities are increasing at a more rapid rate. We have entered a new dimension and as the Earth's energies continue to heighten and quicken, so do our own. With the Earth's shifts, our sensitivities have become more intense. This is a wonderful experience when you know how to work with this new level of energy and take care of yourself in the process. When you learn to ride the wave of energy, you can go with the flow no matter what the speed. It is extremely painful if you are unaware, or winging it, and hoping for the best.

I spoke earlier about how I am sensitive to other people's emotions, energy, and physical pain. It was confusing, frightening, and painful as a child, because I didn't know how to control or manage my abilities. When I learned how to mind my own business and trust my intuitive gift, being sensitive became a blessing in my life. I am now able to tune in to my clients or the energy of an audience and help direct them into a process of healing. I am able to see visions that provide pieces of their healing puzzle. I feel their emotions, physical pain, or energy, and I can help them identify where it is being stored in their physical body. I can sense where root blocks are being held and identify the root cause and shine light on any areas of their life they need to heal. I can literally reach into their energy field and remove blocked energy as long as the client is an active participant who is choosing to heal. I am humbled and honoured to be witness to the miracles of healing from pain, dis-ease, emotional clearings, and so much more. As long as I stay in alignment and trust my intuition, Spirit leads me through every session and everyone is taken care of including me. It is such a gift!

Hearing Dr. Wayne Dyer say "What others think of you is none of your business" felt like such a huge relief, as if a massive weight lifted off my shoulders. Growing up, I wanted to help everyone and save the world. I learned that not everyone is my client and not everyone is meant to resonate with my message, and that's okay. There are many other voices in the world that people can connect with, and I can only trust they find the voice that will inspire and empower them to wake up to the truth about themselves.

When you follow your heart and speak your truth, not everyone is going to understand or agree with what you have to say and that's okay. It is not your job to convince anyone. It is not up to you whether someone wakes up to their heart's path or not. It is up to you to walk your path, follow your heart, and shine your light as brightly as you can. Marianne Williamson writes, "When we let our own light shine we unconsciously give other people permission to do the same." Instead of focusing on the one person you can't convince or who doesn't like what you have to say, focus on the many more who are waiting for your message, your insight, and your love.

When you are in a group or public place, it is essential that your energy is grounded and that you keep your energy field clear of anyone else's. When my energy is grounded, I am standing with unshakeable confidence. I feel solid in my body and clear in my message. Realizing the importance of grounding my energy was pivotal for me and made the biggest difference. I have included a grounding exercise in this chapter.

When I first began offering energy healing and yoga therapy sessions, I would walk away feeling tired and depleted. I would need to take some time in between sessions to recover. Sometimes, I would look at my reflection in my studio mirrors and see the colour draining from my face and the dark circles forming around my eyes as the session continued. I learned from a Reiki Master that our energy is unique to us, like our own DNA. When I was working with clients, I so badly wanted to help them that I started to give them my own energy instead of channeling divine energy clearly through me. She told me that not only am I harming myself and draining my own energy, but that the client couldn't use my energy. Essentially, I was throwing my energy away. I immediately began to practise awareness and the minute I felt a slight drain in my energy, I shifted my awareness to my crown chakra and invited a flow of source energy to flow through me. I became the vessel, allowing the energy to come through me, instead of from me. I no longer felt depleted after giving a session.

I began to see that every interaction becomes an exchange of giving and receiving, and it doesn't have to leave me feeling depleted. Also, it is important to no longer take on other people's issues (positive or negative). Our energies can dance together, but not get tangled up. When I work with a client, or even when I am speaking to an audience of any size, I see it as an exchange. I am sharing the message from my heart and I am receiving from the audience as well. This is the natural order of the Universe. You cannot give without receiving, except when you are not open to receiving. When you are not open to receive, the message, energy, or abundance goes into a bank beside you, until you are ready to make a withdrawal. The way I see it is that many people have rich, overflowing spiritual banks beside them, but never know they can simply make a withdrawal. I often let the Universe know I am making a withdrawal from my spiritual bank and depositing it into my earth bank. This is one way to let the Universe know you are open to receive. I always follow it with deep gratitude in my heart.

> Many people have rich, overflowing spiritual banks beside them, but never know they can simply make a withdrawal.

Another essential tool to practise is clearing your energy field after an exchange, especially if you feel like you let someone else's issues or energy in unintentionally. Remember I mentioned our energies can only dance, but there are times when something we witness affects us deeply and we take on other people's stuff without realizing it. Sometimes others will unconsciously plug into our energy field in an attempt to feel better and raise their vibration to our level. In other words, they want what we have. I have included some tools here to help you protect your precious energy so you can be witness or support for others without sacrificing your own energy and resources.

♥ Heart Work: Protecting Your Precious Energy

Grounding:

The same way a car battery needs to be grounded to function properly, our energy needs to be grounded to function effectively. When practising this tool for the first time, sit in a chair with your feet flat on the floor. Barefoot is best. Later, this can be done sitting, standing, or lying on your back.

~ Feel your feet in contact with the surface beneath you. Imagine your feet are like magnets attracted to the pull of the Earth's magnetic field. Or you can imagine yourself at the beach and your feet are sinking into the sand. Feel the sand surrounding your feet and moving in between your toes. Imagine a solid connection between the Earth and your entire body through your feet.

Cleansing Your Energy Field:

This is helpful when you are leaving a negative environment or if you would like to ensure you take nothing negative home with you from any public gathering or meeting. I used to set this intention every time I left my mind-body studio and I often do it at night before bed. You may find this easier to visualize while standing in the shower and letting the actual water do the cleansing.

~ Imagine a beautiful shower of white light washing over you and all around you. Set the intention to allow any and all negative energy cords or plugs, thoughts or emotions, to wash away easily and effortlessly.

Bubble of Harmony:

This tool is effective for keeping your energy separate from others. It also acts like a filter, allowing love and light in, and reflecting back negative energy. Since integrating this tool, I can be witness to a negative person or environment, without taking the negative energy on or into my field.

~ Imagine a beautiful bubble of light surrounding you, extending about one foot in all directions including below your feet. Set an intention that this brilliant membrane acts as a filter allowing in love and light only, and repelling any negativity. In an extremely negative environment, you can imagine a double bubble of two layers around you.

I encourage you to practise these three tools daily in the beginning. Eventually, they will automatically be in effect without your conscious effort. If you would like to learn more about your energy field and chakra balancing, and receive downloadable guided meditations leading you through these and other energy tools, you can check out my program—"Protecting Your Precious Energy"—at www.heartledliving.com.

As you learn to hold your light and shine brightly in this world, you will illuminate the path for others to do the same. Imagine how bright the world will be when we are all holding our lights and being full expressions of love.

Chapter 4

Heart Led Living Principle ~ Take Inspired Action Only

Everyone is capable of taking action, but it takes a deep level of trust and infinite patience to take inspired action only. Society teaches us to value "being busy", and most people are so constantly doing that, they forget life is designed to be experienced, savoured, and appreciated. Inspired action involves surrendering everything and letting Spirit take the lead. It means waiting patiently for that soft nudge and whisper from your heart saying, "Go now."

> Inspired action involves surrendering everything and letting Spirit take the lead.

People often judge procrastination as a bad thing, but, if I am not inspired to take action, I do nothing. I have learned that if I am guided to do nothing, then that leads to everything. Yes, it is true; sometimes doing nothing is everything. In fact, just recently I was inspired to lie down on the couch and do nothing for two hours. I had moments of resistance, but I finally surrendered. When I was guided to get up and check my email, I had made $500 in sales. Yes, I made $500 doing nothing. The biggest challenge here is discernment.

This chapter will help you understand and feel the difference between ego-encouraged action and Spirit-inspired action.

Our Only Goal

So many people encourage us to set goals. The challenge is that goal-setting is a logical process in our mind and it takes us out of our heart. Most of us are taught to think about goals we would like to achieve. It brings us right into our minds. The ego loves goals and can be very convincing when it comes to thinking about what we need or want. If you want to achieve goals you need to ensure those goals are heart-led. In other words, are they "heart goals" or "head goals"? Unless the goal comes from the heart into the mind, you are going to be forcing and it will be hard work rather than HEART work.

In *Heart Led Living*, we redefine goals and recommend setting heart-led intentions. This means we let go of what we think we should or shouldn't do and let our hearts lead us toward what we are meant to do or achieve. In *Heart Led Living*, we have only one goal and this is alignment with Spirit. This means we open our minds to receive an intention, follow our hearts, and trust our intuition. We have one goal, which is alignment with Spirit, and we set intentions based on what we are guided to set.

I have had this book in my heart for years. I knew I was going to write another book incorporating stories from my life, but I never knew when or how it was going to happen. I just knew it was in my heart. When I first met Julie Salisbury from Influence Publishing, I told her my ideas and what I thought the book would be about. I felt an immediate connection to her and everything she said resonated deep in my heart. I was guided to attend a weekend workshop with Julie and, by Sunday night, I had my title, bio, synopsis, chapters, and chapter subtitles all mapped out, and I moved on to sign a publishing contract with her.

When I sat down to start writing, everything inside me was resisting writing Chapter One. I thought it was because it was a heavy and emotional beginning. As I read through the chapter titles I was really drawn to Chapters Seven and Eight so I began writing there. This is not how I would usually do any writing: I wrote my previous books from beginning to end; but I followed my intuition and trusted the process without judgment. Chapter Seven was very therapeutic for me and I felt like I purged a great deal of grief. I sent it to Julie to review. She was guided not to give me any feedback and she encouraged me to keep going. So I started writing Chapter Eight and it flowed easily and effortlessly. It was fun and easy to write, and I finished writing five thousand words within five hours.

As I went back to my original Chapter One, I felt this huge, heavy weight in my heart and so much resistance. When I spoke to Julie after she read Chapter Eight, she said, "Sue, I believe this is your book." My heart jumped with excitement about the idea of expanding on the ideas and concepts in Chapter Eight, as she showed me how to incorporate my personal stories within the content. And voila, the book you are now reading came into my awareness and my writing has been easy, fun, and flowing ever since. Julie and I were both following our intuition and leading with our hearts. That is why she was able to help me see the real book that was meant to come through me. As I released what I thought I was going to write, what I was meant to write started flowing through my heart, into my fingers, and onto paper with ease and grace. I became the vessel, or faucet, and allowed the message to flow through me.

When we completely surrender a book, relationships, music, writing, food, work, family, everything all over to Spirit, and set an intention to be a clear and perfect channel, then we allow Spirit to lead us every moment of every day. And that, my friends, is what *Heart Led Living* is all about.

♥ Heart Work: Aligning With Spirit Is the Only Goal

Setting Heart-Led Intentions:

Find stillness and silence. Take eight deep breaths as you rest with your eyes closed and invite your mind to become clear. Imagine that you could drop your awareness into your heart for guidance. Ask your heart, "What is my intention?" Don't think about anything, simply allow the answer to pop into your mind in the form of words, or a vision, or image. You may even receive a feeling of gratitude or joy. This is a great exercise to start your day with. It will help strengthen your intuition around setting heart-led intentions.

I Don't Do Busy

I am sure you have heard the saying "we are human beings not human doings". When we are busy doing a task it is common to worry about what still needs to get done. Thoughts of worry, anxiety, and fear, and other meaningless thoughts fill our mind. Have you ever had a to do list running through your mind as you are on autopilot doing the dishes or laundry? This is actually a clever distraction tactic of our ego thought system. The more distracted we are, the less likely we are to hear our heart's guidance. When we practise being fully present and aware of what we are doing, we are in alignment and able to tune into our intuitive heart for guidance.

I first became aware of this when I observed the peace I felt doing the dishes while on vacation with my family. I was fully present, doing the dishes without worrying about what I needed to do next. I was on vacation and we had no timeline. My mind was calm and I felt such peace and content. I felt like I had all the time in the world. Time seemed to stand still. When I returned home and back into my daily routine and busy schedule, I found myself irritated and rushing to get the dishes done. Even though we have a dishwasher, it seemed to take forever and my mind was consumed with thoughts of worry around all the other things I needed to get done before bedtime.

When we worry, we feel like we are doing something. Society teaches us to take pride in being busy. Our ego would have us believe that by keeping busy, we are being productive, but the truth is we are completely distracting ourselves from our internal guidance and intuition. When worry, fear, and anxiety fill your mind, you are less likely to be able to hear insight. You are also choosing to align with ego as your teacher. If you want to learn to hear and trust your intuition, then it is essential that you practise being fully present and be willing to do nothing.

A more accurate phrase than "being busy" would be "doing busy". People are so busy "doing" that they are not living. They are not thriving and enjoying life; they are surviving and too busy "doing" to enjoy each moment.

Often when a client calls me for support they start out with, "I know you're busy, but ..." My response is, "I don't do busy." I used to do busy, but not anymore. When you become witness and fully aware of what you are doing while you are doing it, you are being fully present to life. When you are fully present to life as it unfolds, you are in alignment, and you are able to tune in and feel your intuition in everything you do. Our ego wants us to stay busy, going from one thing to the next, because then we remain distracted from life as it truly unfolds in each precious moment. What if there were a way to rest in the "busyness"? What if I told you that you could get more done if you stopped multitasking and focused on the task you were guided to do in that moment?

One of the days I set aside to write this book became a powerful lesson in alignment, ease, and flow. I managed to get more done in one day than I ever thought possible. And the best part is it was incredibly easy, light, and fun. I wrote at least three thousand words for my book, vacuumed the entire house, did laundry, answered emails, cleaned out the goat house and chicken coops, gave my horse a cold rinse with water along with some apples, and kisses of course, had lunch on the deck in the sun, meditated, did yoga, played with the kittens, organized and put out the garbage and recycling, fed and watered all my critters, and it was only 5:00 p.m. This is what I call Heart Led Living. Every moment I am in alignment and tuned into what my heart guides me to do, it is as if time slows down to accommodate all that I am meant to complete. Every moment I would ask my heart, "What would you have me do now?" and I was literally led to each and every task. While I was performing each task, I was fully present without thoughts. My mind was clear and I was simply being present to each moment as it unfolded. Every moment became a gift.

> Every moment I am in alignment and tuned into what my heart guides me to do, it is as if time slows down to accommodate all that I am meant to complete.

♥ Heart Work: Be Still and Do Nothing

While you may think this exercise needs no explanation, I know how hard it can be to stop and be still. When I first started doing yoga, I found the first minute of stillness to be physically painful and mentally challenging. I may have found stillness in my body, but my mind was racing and my body was screaming at me in pain. I recognized that my body was always in that amount of pain, but I had never stopped to listen to it.

- Find stillness in a position in which you can relax your body but stay awake.
- Focus on your breath for at least eight breath cycles to help you become fully present. Remember, your breath is a reliable link to the present moment.

- Ask yourself, "What is happening now?" and observe without judgment. You may notice physical sensations, emotions, thoughts, energy, colours, images, words, etc. There is no need to change anything, simply observe whatever comes into your awareness.

- After about ten minutes, imagine you can clear your mind and drop your awareness into your heart, and ask, "What would you have me do now?" Be open and curious for an answer from your intuitive heart. For some people, the answer comes in quickly, so I often recommend you go with the first thing that pops into your mind. As you practise, you will become better at discerning between what you are guided to do and what your mind thinks you should do.

- Follow your guidance, and as you do, practise being fully present to that experience by asking yourself, "What is happening now?" Whether you are guided to wash dishes, go for a walk, remain in stillness, or perform a chore, set your intention to be fully present so you can practise "being" while doing.

Forgiveness Is For Giving

Most people believe forgiveness is something we do for another or something we ask of another. In *Heart Led Living*, forgiveness is a gift we give to our self, first, then to others. A lack of forgiveness is a toxin in our body. It lurks deep in the body as the dark shadow of resentment, anger, guilt, and/or shame. The energy of these unresolved emotions can eat us up inside, causing dis-ease in the body, such as cancer. Forgiving someone for something they did to you is not about saying that what they did was right or okay. In fact, it is not about another person. Forgiveness is about you taking your power back and freeing yourself from past trauma and past regret. Forgiveness begins with creating awareness and space for healing what no longer serves us, and releasing the toxins we are carrying from our past.

We heal in layers, like an onion; some layers are thicker than others. Some layers are easy and others make you cry. There may be times when emotions seem to come out of left field. When you create space for the expression of those emotions, you can heal another layer. The challenge is we tend to deny, hold back, or suppress those emotions. As the wise cartoon ogre Shrek says, "Better out than in." When you can create space to allow the old trauma to come to the surface to be released, you will free yourself from it once and for all. We never have to heal the same layer more than once. When you heal it once, it is done. Your ego wants you to be afraid that the process never ends. I have had clients tell me they are afraid that if they let themselves cry they will never stop. I assure you the tears will end and you will feel relief on the other side of crying. Emotions, thoughts, beliefs, and physical trauma are held in the body in the form of energy and they need to be released in order to heal. Emotion is energy in motion. Sometimes it is easy and other times it is more challenging. Either way, I encourage you to give it to Spirit for healing. That is what forgiving means. It is for giving over and asking for healing.

> We never have to heal the same layer
> more than once.

Recently, I woke up feeling depressed. I felt a huge burden and weight in my physical body, as thoughts of suicide and depression came into my mind. Years ago, I would have panicked and done what I could do to numb the emotional pain using food, alcohol, or other harmful substances.

I suddenly remembered an evening when I had woken up slumped in my living room chair. My head and body had felt heavy from the amount of alcohol still in my blood. I had partied all night and most of the next morning. I hadn't eaten anything for seven days and my only calories during that time were from alcohol. I had looked around to find I was completely alone in the dark. A wave of shame, guilt, and disgust had washed over me and tears had filled my eyes. "What am I doing? How much worse does it need to get before I stop?" I felt like I was dying inside. I realized, in that moment, that I no longer had control over alcohol or my eating disorder. I was quickly spiralling out of control. I felt an intense pain deep in my soul and it was like a knife through my heart.

I recalled watching myself pick up the phone and start dialling. It was as if I was floating above my body witnessing a movie play out below me. A young woman answered the phone, "You have reached the help line. How can I help you?"

With tears flowing down my cheeks, my hand shaking nervously, and my voice cracking with fear, I asked, "Can you please tell me one thing I can do for fun that doesn't involve alcohol, because I can't think of anything?" The woman remained quiet. She had no answer for me. I waited a couple more seconds and hung up the phone. I felt defeated once again. I turned to the only support I knew that would give me relief at the time; I poured another glass of wine. At the bottom of the glass my pain subsided. Instead of recognizing the pain as a call for healing, as an opportunity to release the burden I was carrying, I chose to have another drink and numb it once again. A year later, I received help for my eating disorder. Unfortunately, my unhealthy relationship with alcohol continued for several more years. Eventually I learned to enjoy life without alcohol, and fun is something I experience every day as a side effect of being in alignment with Spirit.

Today, I see pain and discomfort as opportunities to heal layers of old trauma. I don't use any vices to numb out the pain; I choose to face it with compassion and self-love. So recently, when I woke up feeling depressed, I knew it was old wounds coming to the surface. I was able to be witness without judgment, as I felt waves of memories, in which I had hit rock bottom and felt completely helpless, wash over me. I could see myself stuck in a hole with no way out. This lasted a couple of hours and I wasn't guided to do anything other than sit, be fully present, and allow all the emotions to surface. I waited for inspired action even though it was uncomfortable. I was finally guided to complete the "emptying process." All my past physical, mental, and emotional memories of contemplating suicide and feeling depressed came up and out. I created space as my body started to shake and tears filled my eyes. Within minutes, the shaking stopped and I felt a renewed sense of joy. I was being held in this brilliant blanket of love and I felt as light as a feather.

As we give everything over to Spirit for healing, we set an intention to forgive anyone and anything that needs forgiving, including our self. While the FEAR process in Chapter Three works really well, I have also included an exercise in forgiveness below for you to practise.

♥ Heart Work: Forgiveness

Writing a letter is one of the most powerful tools for forgiveness. Keep in mind these letters are for your eyes only. Forgiveness is an internal process, which may or may not lead to talking to someone else. I often encourage my clients to write three letters using pen on paper.

- The first one is meant to express and empty out all your thoughts, fears, and feelings about what happened. I often refer to this one as the "Eff You" letter.
- This allows the second letter to be more effective; this is a letter of forgiveness toward the other person.
- The third letter is a letter of forgiveness to self. Keep in mind you may also need to express regret, disappointment, and anger toward yourself, in order to reach a level of authentic forgiveness.

Be patient and create a sacred space for authentic expression. The letters are never meant to be shared. Many clients burn them as a symbol of letting go and moving on. Follow your heart. If you are meant to speak to the person you have forgiven, you will be given the guidance around that. No attachment. In my experience, in most cases it has been unnecessary. Remember, forgiveness is about freeing yourself and releasing toxic burdens from your heart, body, and mind.

Practising Infinite Patience

In *Heart Led Living*, we take inspired action only. There is nothing to do unless there is something we are guided to do. Therefore, following our intuitive heart takes infinite patience. Sometimes, we need to sit in non-action until clear guidance comes in. Spirit works in the present moment only and guides us to take each step as it appears in front of us. If you are walking up a staircase the only way to get to the top is to take the step that is front of you. One step at a time, one moment at a time, one breath at a time. For many people, sitting in non-action and the unknown are points of weakness for the ego to come in. It feeds the mind with thoughts convincing us that we need to know now and suddenly impatience, confusion, and doubt fill our mind and body.

> We never have to heal the same layer more than once.

One of the foundation mindsets in *Heart Led Living* is "I don't know and it's okay". This deep level of acceptance and surrender allows us to get out of the way and lets Spirit lead us in every moment. We make peace with where we are and we surrender to following our heart. From our human perspective, it looks like nothing is happening. But from our higher self or Spirit's perspective, perfection playing out. The Universe is orchestrating everything and everyone we need to align with to fulfill our heart's desire. The resistance comes in when we question the timing, the "how", or the outcome. When you trust in the process, you will experience miracles that go beyond what your mind could ever begin to imagine.

A year after my son was born, my husband and I started trying to get pregnant again. When it didn't happen right away, I felt frustration rising within me and thought there has to be another way. In Dr. Wayne Dyer's book, *Inspiration* (published by Hay House in 2006)—you will have gathered I admire Dr. Dyer greatly—he says that "being inspired" means "being in spirit". It was exactly what I needed to hear. I found the inspiration and trusted my intuition to start teaching "Yoga for Fertility" classes. Initially, the classes were for me, yet within two months, I opened Family Passages Mind Body Studio. It was the first studio in Canada to specialize in fertility yoga, supporting women through conception, pregnancy, and postpartum. It was a gift for women and couples, and I witnessed many miracles.

After three years of trying to conceive, I became reflective and began to question my own fertility journey. While the yoga had helped me conceive my son, why wasn't it working this time? I never questioned whether I was qualified to teach, because many of my clients were getting pregnant. One answer that came was that I wasn't practising yoga for fertility for myself; I was teaching it. I was the instructor not one of the students. There was something else I was missing, yet I still felt a yearning for another child. At the same time, I was experiencing more health challenges and my liver started to show signs of distress by showing up as jaundice of my skin.

In meditation one morning, I received insight that it would not be good self-care to have another pregnancy. In fact, I was shown that my body could not handle it. I had to let go of the idea of getting pregnant again. There was a lot of grief, sadness, and loss, but I came out the other side and made a choice for self-love and self-care. In hindsight, I realized that it was all purposeful. If I hadn't wanted to conceive another child through pregnancy, I wouldn't have started teaching yoga for fertility and opened my studio. My heart filled with gratitude for the insight.

It was at that point that I tuned into a deep desire to adopt a little girl from Africa. I couldn't have had this insight before. I had previously wanted to have another pregnancy, but not to adopt. Yet, with the choice to become pregnant off the table, I was open to a new perspective. Again the insight came in with divine timing. I had to go through all the pain of letting go of getting pregnant to come to this clarity. Many people, including my husband, asked me, "Why Africa?"

I didn't have any reasonable or logical answer. For as long as I can remember, I have always felt a heart connection to Africa. It was just a feeling and knowing deep in my heart that I was meant to help children in Africa. I started to feel that there was a child in Africa that I was meant to love.

My husband and I started on the road to adoption. It was crystal clear for three years until the day we received our final home-study report from our adoption counsellor. Something shifted in my heart. It took a few months of self-reflection and conversations with my husband when I realized it was time to close the door on adopting. After a few weeks of aligning my head with my heart, I removed our name from the African adoption wait list. I remained open and curious, because I still felt there was a deep connection to Africa in some way.

Suddenly, a bigger picture entered my awareness. I saw myself supporting many children in Africa, not by bringing them to Canada, but by empowering them in their own country. I realized I am not meant to adopt one little girl but instead I am meant to inspire and empower many. That is when I was shown a vision of my "Heart Led Living Foundation." While the foundation is still in its early conception and infancy, the vision I have received is heart-warming and exciting. It was through practising infinite patience that I was able to heal throughout my fertility journey and be open to the guidance in each moment. I remained curious and open to the spiritual re-directions. I trusted that it was all purposeful. In hindsight, if I hadn't gone through my own fertility challenges with my miscarriage, trouble conceiving my son, the inability to conceive another child, and exploring the road to adoption, I wouldn't have created all the programs to support women and couples all around the world. Even though my fertility journey has come to an end, I continue to help couples unite with the children they are meant to have. If you or someone you know needs fertility support, visit www.familypassages.ca

There is no way I could have guessed the purpose of all this. I was able to practise infinite patience because I embraced the idea that "I don't know and it's okay". I trusted that everything was playing out for the highest good of all, including for me. I trust that my "Heart Led Living Foundation" will come into fruition when it is most purposeful. I continue to practise patience and I am wide open to any guidance or inspired action. I trust in divine timing, knowing that I will be shown what I need to see when I need to see it, and for that I am deeply grateful.

♥ Heart Work: A Five-Step Process to Seek Guidance From Spirit

This process will help you tune into and trust your guidance. It is also an exercise in discernment, so you can be sure the insight you are getting is fully aligned with Spirit and not ego in disguise. When you know you are in alignment with Spirit, it is easier to practise infinite patience, because you can trust that you will be taken care of and that it is all-purposeful.

Step 1: I Ask

~ The quality of the answers you receive will depend on the quality of the answers you seek. Wording is essential. Ask, "What am I meant to learn from this experience?" or "What would you have me know at this time?"

Step 2: I Listen

~ I find it curious that a lot of people are asking for answers, but fail to actually listen. Stop, be still, and open your mind to receive the answer in whatever way you are most likely to receive it. Be curious without attachment to any answer. Listen with your inner ear and allow the answer to come into your awareness as an image, feeling, thought, word, vision, sense, knowing, or otherwise.

Step 3: I Feel

~ Once you receive an answer, feel into it. Bring it into your heart and mind, and notice how your body feels. If it is true guidance from your heart, you will feel light, expanded, and/or joyous. If it is ego in disguise, you will feel heavy, tight, and/or uncertain. You are feeling for the "heart yes" or "heart no." This step of discernment is one that people often skip. I promise, if you take the time to tune into the feeling, you will save yourself a lot of time and energy.

Step 4: I Follow

~ Remember, when you receive clear guidance from your intuitive heart, you need to follow it, no matter what. That includes whether it makes sense to you at the time or not, and also when it doesn't make sense to others. In *Heart Led Living*, we practise obedience and set an intention to follow our intuition always.

Step 5: I Move

~ When you receive guidance you may want to jump up and take action immediately. Remember Spirit works on a "need to know" basis. We may receive guidance without inspired action. Sometimes we need to marinate our mind in the new insight before we are guided to move. This strengthens our faith and trust, so we can walk step by step with divine courage. This ensures that we are in full alignment with Spirit as our teacher and guide.

Spirit works on a "need to know" basis.

The ego loves to take insight and fill in the rest of the story to move you into ego-encouraged action. Practise infinite patience and you will feel clear heart-led action.

Chapter 5

Heart Led Living Principle ~ Fill Your Heart First

Society teaches us to give, give, and give some more, until we are empty and depleted. We are taught that if we are not giving we are being selfish. This leads to feeling depleted and it will eventually show up as dis-ease. When we understand the importance of filling our hearts first and giving from the overflow, everyone is taken care of including us. There is no sacrifice. It is only a win-win outcome. Everyone benefits. Everyone thrives. Everyone wins. This chapter is going to shed light on anything and everything that is blocking your ability to receive and give with harmony, grace, and ease. As you fill your heart first, you will discover an abundant energy and life force that enables you to do more than you ever thought possible. This is the key to having the most positive impact on the healing of our planet. It all begins within your heart.

Practising Vibrant Self-Care

If you don't take care of yourself, you can't take care of others. We are taught that self-care is selfish. It is not selfish; self-care is self-love. When we love ourselves enough to practise vibrant self-care, we teach others how to do the same.

Self-care is about taking care of your basic needs, like eating, sleeping, and drinking water. Vibrant self-care requires self-awareness, non-judgment, and commitment.

Before I realized I had cancer in my body, I was working hard and ignoring the physical signals of resistance. I remember for at least six months before I closed my studio, after nearly every private session with clients, I felt drained. I couldn't rest much between sessions, because I booked myself back-to-back to accommodate as many clients as I could. I found it hard to turn people away because I really wanted to help everyone. This came at a great cost, which eventually led to me taking an entire year to heal and restore my health and wellbeing. I learned from that experience. I no longer take on every client that calls. I only say "Yes" to those that I am guided to work with. Today when my body is telling me to rest, I rest. I see it as a time of restoration and integration. Sometimes I rest for an entire day, but more often it is ten minutes up to a few hours of lying on my back in meditation and I feel energized and renewed.

One of the seven universal laws is the Law of Rhythm and Harmony, which governs that everything is moving to and fro, flowing in and out, swinging backward and forward. There is always a reaction to every action. Like the ebb and flow of the tides, there are natural highs and lows in life. Even in a woman's menstrual cycle there are fluctuations in energy and hormone levels. This is a natural occurrence in nature, as well as within our bodies. When women are menstruating, or as I prefer to call it "celebrating our cycle", it is a time of rest and restoration. When women give themselves permission to rest during their cycle, it becomes a time for self-reflection. When we understand this law we learn to go with the flow and rest in the ebb. If we resist or judge the natural ebb or flow, we experience the pain of resistance and immediately align with ego.

♥ Heart Work: Riding "the Low"

The next time you feel a low in energy, remain curious without judgment. Give yourself permission to rest and restore your energy. There have been days when I felt the low but kept pushing through; as a result, I had two to three even more challenging days that followed. Now I realize that if I take time to lie on my back, to allow my body and spine time for integration and restoration, it only takes a couple of hours or at most half a day to feel better. Our nervous system is constantly receiving information from our environment and when we take the time to rest the spine, we allow the processing and integration on a physical, mental, and emotional level. For example, if we experience a traumatic or stressful event during the day, we can set an intention to release any leftover dense energy or anxiety while we rest. At the same time, the physical body is releasing the energy and experience of the trauma through the nervous system. If you wish to understand this concept more and go deeper into the physiology and science behind it, I recommend the book *Beyond Body, Beyond Mind* by Dr Sukhi Muker (published by CreateSpace Independent Publishing Platform in 2012).

I give you full permission to rest. Here are some things I do that help me ride the low: listen to a guided meditation; watch an inspiring movie; read a book; sit in nature; swing in a hammock; take a nap; practise restorative yoga poses (e.g. legs up the wall pose, child's pose); rest quietly with my eyes closed and focus on my breath.

Follow your heart; I promise it will lead you to your secret recipe for riding the low back into the high. Remember, that by being nonjudgmental and by practising infinite patience, you will quicken the healing time required for integration.

Stop and Breathe

Our breath is a reliable link to the present moment. It is the most powerful yet the most underutilized tool. When we focus on our breath to become present, we give our mind something to focus on. The mind loves to observe, analyze, and figure things out. When you observe each inhale and exhale, you give your mind a job and it will quieten down. It can help you regain control of your mind.

> The mind loves to observe, analyze, and figure things out.
> When you observe each inhale and exhale, you give your
> mind a job and it will quieten down.

I now realize that, for the longest time, I taught about finding space between our thoughts even though I never really experienced it. My ego had my thoughts coming and going like a storm, keeping me in confusion and uncertainty. I had so much going on in my mind, it was like there was no "off" switch. Our mind is a reflection of our environment and at that time, my schedule was just as busy as my mind. After years of teaching step aerobics, kickboxing, and other high-energy fitness classes, I started teaching yoga. It was a gentle transition, because sitting in stillness was painful, physically and emotionally. Yet intuitively, I knew I needed to slow things down. The slow, restorative "Fertility Yoga" class I taught slowed down my body, and I was then able to slow down my mind.

I remember once when I was talking to my husband, I went quiet for about fifteen seconds. He asked what I was thinking and I said something like, "Well, I was talking about Lisa coming for a visit and I realized I needed to get some groceries. Then I thought I really should clean the bathrooms and remembered that I also need to get dog food. The dogs are so muddy right now we should really bathe them. If only it would stop raining for a few days, the ground would dry up. I still need to plant the garden. Boy, am I feeling hungry. I wonder what we should eat for lunch. Perhaps I can go pick up something when I get groceries before Lisa arrives. I may need to get some gas on the way and I still need to stop at the post office and the bank."

His eyes were wide as he looked at me with surprise. He asked, "You thought all of that in fifteen seconds?"

A few days later, we were chatting again and he stopped talking and gazed out the window. I curiously asked what he was thinking and he said, "Nothing."

I questioned with disbelief, "What do you mean nothing? How can you possibly have nothing in your mind? Is it blank?"

His response made me laugh out loud, as he started humming the theme music for the circus. Yes. His mind was blank. We still look back at those times and laugh at just how ridiculously busy my mind was and how peacefully quiet his was.

Today, I can sit in silent meditation and my mind is quiet most of the time. There is definitely more space between my thoughts. My mind is a reflection of the teacher I am choosing at the time, ego or Spirit. When I am in alignment with Spirit, there is quiet and a sense of peace and calm in my mind and body. Instead, ego busily fills my mind with useless thoughts and negativity. I use breath work a lot when my mind is racing into fear, worry, or anxiety. Intentional breathing is one tool that helps me turn my thoughts off and return to alignment with Spirit almost instantly. When you have space in your mind you tap into an unlimited potential and a clean slate to receive guidance from Spirit. My best downloads from Spirit are just after I finish my yoga practice and open my journal. In stillness and silence, wisdom and insight come pouring in.

♥ Heart Work: The Healing Power of the Breath

Observing Your Breath

Take a moment to notice your breath. Notice each inhale and exhale. Observe the length of your breath in and compare it to the length of your breath out. No judgment, simply observe. Where is there a restriction in your breath? Where in your chest and lungs do you notice an ease and flow of your breath? Now take a deep breath in and exhale with a sigh.

Deep breathing can also turn off our parasympathetic nervous system (flight or fight response) and turn on our sympathetic nervous system (rest and restore). By simply taking ten deep breaths in and out of your nose, you can send a message to your mind that you are safe and all is well. That signal of safety automatically turns on your sympathetic nervous system once again.

Exhale Negative, Inhale Positive

Next time you feel anxious or worried, imagine yourself exhaling the negative emotions. Visualize the negative thoughts, or feelings, or worry leaving your body with your exhale. You may see it as a cloud of smoke or specks of black. You don't even need an image; simply set the intention and you will feel a shift. As you create space, begin to inhale peace and calm, or whatever feeling you wish to invite into your body and mind. Imagine that it is easy to bring in the energy of calm. Tune into a memory of feeling calm and allow it to fill your body. You will be pleasantly surprised at how powerful your breath can be when you use it purposefully.

Practising Soul Care

Take a moment to reflect on your ability to give and receive. Do you find it easier to give or is it easier for you to receive? Most of us, especially women, find it easier to give. We are natural givers. We are also taught by society that giving is the right thing to do. Today, I recognize that giving and receiving are equally important; but we are rarely taught the importance of receiving. In fact, many of us feel unworthy of receiving.

For years, I was practising what I thought was extreme self-care, as I have said. In my awakening I realized the focus should not just be on self-care; it should be on self-care and soul care.

Focus on self-care and soul care.

Soul care is about filling your heart first, not just a little bit, but actually filling it all the way to the tippy top. Maya Angelou speaks about filling your cup and giving from the overflow. I like to imagine filling my heart first and giving from the overflow, because the image personalizes it. It brings it into my body, mind, and soul.

If you take the time you need to fill your heart to the point of overflow, you will have enough energy for everyone else including you. YES, including YOU! You must be part of this equation. In the beginning, you might feel selfish, but when you see how much more you have to give others, you will understand the value.

Self-care and soul care are about self-love, as well as love for others. When you have a sacred soul-care practice in place, and rest when you are guided to rest, you will have enough for yourself and everyone else. Visualize a beautiful fountain in your heart with a constant flow of water coming up and overflowing all around your heart, and entering back into the bottom of your heart. It is a renewable source that you top up daily to keep the levels high. Not only will you have sustainable energy, you will experience vibrant health. People, especially children, learn by watching what others do. When you practise soul care and self-care, you teach them, by example, that your health and well-being matter, and so do theirs.

♥ Heart Work: Soul Care and Vibrant Self-Care Rituals

Creating vibrant soul care and self-care begins with discovering rituals that feed your soul and fill your heart. Here are some of my daily rituals to give you some ideas. If any of them resonate deep in your heart then I suggest you follow that cue.

Meditation:

You can begin with a guided meditation practice and, once you get accustomed to sitting in stillness, you can move to stillness and silence. Start with five to ten minutes and stay tuned into your intuition. You may be guided to a longer meditation practice. As a member in our *Heart Led Living* community, you receive several meditations you can download and use to create a daily practice. I often listen to my own recorded meditations to realign with Spirit and heal any nigglings or leftovers from my day.

Yoga:

I experience yoga as meditation in movement. If you feel drawn to starting a yoga practice, initially you can watch a video or take some classes to get comfortable with yoga postures. You can do ten to fifteen minutes, or you may even be guided to do just one yoga pose. Let your body lead you and notice how you feel before, during, and after each yoga pose. It is not about doing it perfectly; rather it is about listening to your body and respecting the cues it is gives you. I teach my students to find the point in the posture where they feel challenged yet supported. In our *Heart Led Living* membership, we have "Heart Led Yoga" classes you can access online at www.heartledliving.com for you to begin a heart-led yoga practice.

Authentic Journaling:

This is essentially a conversation with Spirit. I begin my journaling with, "Dear Spirit." I express gratitude and appreciation, and then I often ask a question or ask for insight around a specific situation. If I don't have anything I need guidance on, I ask, "What would you have me know in this moment?" and I am wide open to any wisdom that comes through my pen onto paper. I do suggest you use pen and paper, and not your computer. Without the interference of any electronics, you can more directly connect with Spirit.

Hot Lemon Water:

I start every day off with half a fresh lemon squeezed into hot water to help aid my digestion. While acidic in nature, lemons provide an alkalinizing effect on the body. Foods that produce a more alkaline and less acidic effect on the body create a more favourable environment for healing.

Make the juice fresh each morning and drink it within twenty minutes. Follow it up with an alkaline mouth rinse to neutralize the acidic effect of the lemon juice on your teeth. This will help prevent damage to your tooth enamel.

High Quality Supplements:

I choose to take the highest quality supplements, produced by USANA, a company with integrity and uncompromising quality control. I was introduced to them by Dr. Christiane Northrup. I deeply trust USANA Health Sciences with my health and the health of my family, and I have seen amazing physical improvements from using their products. I have tried many supplements during my fitness and wellness career. I have tried plant-based ones, organic ones, expensive ones, and everything in between; nothing ever seemed to work as deeply as the USANA products. These are the first and only products that I actually feel make a positive difference in my health. Without them, I wouldn't have been able to heal the cancer in my body as quickly as I did. In my opinion, the only thing that is missing on the label of this product is LOVE.

If you would like to learn more about USANA supplements, you can visit my website at www.suedumais.usana.com or contact me and I can help you decide which products your body needs. In the interests of full disclosure, I can tell you that I love and trust these products so much that I have decided to become a distributor to benefit my clients.

High Vibration Foods:

Every food vibrates at a different level. Food that is processed or that contains harmful ingredients is naturally lower in vibration. Food that is closest to its original form will be higher. For example, fresh, local, and organic fruit has a higher vibration and carries more nutrients than a fruit product that was picked early and shipped from another country or region of your country. Having said that, I have had some processed foods and products that are high in vibration. It is all based on the manufacturing process and the intention of the company producing it. You can also change the vibration of a food item simply by setting the intention to raise its vibration before you consume it. This is where saying grace or giving thanks for a meal is effective. It doesn't have to be a religious ritual if you don't practise a religion; but it can become a ritual of gratitude and appreciation for your food.

I choose to eat more vegetables than fruits. I aim for at least ten to twelve veggies and two to three fruit servings each day. I drink green juice and also add a high-vibrating greens powder to my smoothie every morning. I avoid starchy carbs, white processed foods like flour and sugar, and I no longer drink any alcohol.

Pick one area of your nutrition to start and make the change that feels good in your heart. Keep in mind, what is higher vibration for one may be lower for another. If someone currently eats primarily fast foods, then any live food would be a higher vibrating food for them. If you are someone who already eats clean, you may be inspired to start green juicing. For a period of time during my healing, almonds caused gastrointestinal challenges for me. They lowered my vibration as a result. Now I can eat a handful as a source of protein and I feel great.

Follow your intuition and let go of everything you think you know about food. Follow your heart and it will lead you to the changes you need to make. Choosing foods because you are afraid of others is alignment with ego. Avoiding certain foods because that is what you are guided to do is alignment with Spirit.

> Follow your intuition and let go of everything you think you know about food. Follow your heart and it will lead you to the changes you need to make.

Asking for Healing While You Sleep:

If I have an issue I am focused on healing, I often ask for support while I sleep. I ask all my guides and angels to come in and surround me with divine love and healing energy. I set an intention to release anything and everything that is no longer serving me. If you do this every night, sometimes you might feel your sleep is interrupted a bit. If this happens for several nights in a row, you may need to ask Spirit for a break so you can have a restful sleep.

Give It Over:

Anything that comes to the surface for healing during the day, I am willing to explore, express, and release. The moment I notice an upset, I ask for clarity: "Is there anything I need to know about this upset?" I often get an answer or insight, and sometimes it is just old stuff that needs to go. Whatever it is, I release it into the arms of Spirit and ask for healing at the deepest possible level. You can imagine giving it to Spirit or placing it on a platter or even in a garbage can. Make the intention to give it over for healing; that matters most. If there are any physical or emotional expressions necessary, I am fully willing to allow the expressions so I can heal on every level: physically, mentally, emotionally, spiritually, and energetically. Often my body shakes as the energy leaves my body. Other times there are tears for no reason or waves of emotions rising up and out. You don't need to understand it all; just simply be willing to give it over for healing and be wide open for any insight or guidance around it.

Joining:

In *Heart Led Living*, we practise "joining". I have explained this process in Chapter Two.

As you begin to integrate some of these daily rituals into your day, notice how you feel before, during, and after. Continue the rituals until they no longer resonate. As you let one go, often a new one will come into your awareness. Remember, in *Heart Led Living*, we are open to anything and attached to nothing. A tool or daily practice will come in and stay as long as it remains purposeful.

From Selfless Service to Self-Fulfilled Service to the World

Gandhi said, "Be the change you wish to see in the world." He didn't say "live in fear and sacrifice everything you are, hoping that by expending all your life's energy the world will change". Healing the planet begins with healing ourselves. Be the change. If you wish to see more love, then raise the level of love within yourself and you will be able to extend more to others. If you wish to see more compassion, be more compassionate to self and others. If you wish to see more peace on earth, find inner peace and spread the vibration of peace toward others.

Society wants us to believe that healing the world is impossible or that hard work comes with great sacrifice. "Be the change" sounds too simple. But sometimes the truth is that simple. Imagine if we all practised more self-love. Collectively, we would raise the level of love in the world and we would show, by example, that everyone deserves love. Everyone!

The whole idea of giving selfless service to the world doesn't serve anyone when it comes at the cost of sacrificing our own wellness. We are each an extension of one source, and that means we all deserve to feel fulfilled. There are two ways to be of service. One is in alignment with ego and one is in alignment with Spirit. Ego has us give, give, and give some more, until we have nothing left to give. Ego makes us feel guilty for what we have and convinces us that we are being selfish. Ego wants us to feel sad for others and hold their pain in our heart so we suffer along with them. Ego makes us believe that our "having" means someone else goes without.

I used to think that, in order to feel worthy of my success, I had to prove to others how much I had suffered for it. That way others wouldn't think I was being selfish for wanting more in my life. I see others being of service in the world, only in order to prove they are worthy of everything they have. We believe if we help others enough, then we deserve the rewards that come to us in life. In my experience, no matter what I did it was never enough. It is human nature to "want"; the question is are your "wants" ego-driven, or are your "wants" your true heart's desires? Remember, your ego is tricky. Your ego will find any points of weakness and weasel its way in. Your ego is ready and waiting to take you down into a wormhole. Your ego would tell you, "Go help others; be of service to the world. That is the right thing to do." Spirit says, "Love yourself, follow your heart, and you will be of service to the world." The more you love and accept yourself, the more you can love and accept others.

Spirit-inspired service allows us to give from the overflow in our heart. There is no self-sacrifice. There is only love and compassion for self and others. You not only deserve success, abundance, joy, happiness, and to live a life that you love: it is your birthright. And it is the birthright of every one of us. Is everyone meant to have a huge house, new car, and lots of money? No, it is not on everyone's heart path to have large amounts of money. Our heart's path is designed for the awakening and healing of our soul so the amount of money will be purposeful for us. In order to do our heart's work in this world, we need to embrace money. It is okay to make money. In fact, in our society, money is a necessity. Mother Theresa did amazing humanitarian work and lived with very little. At the same time, when people asked Mother Theresa the question, "How can I support you with your cause?" she replied without hesitation, "I need money." She recognized that in order to have a greater impact and help more people she needed more money. I choose to see money as energy; it is to be used in whatever way it is most purposeful. The more I make, the more impact I can have in this world.

> You not only deserve success, abundance, joy, happiness, and to live a life that you love: it is your birthright.

I recently read a blog post written by an old friend and I was shocked to hear his perspective on healing. His blog post was titled "Healing is a Gift". He explained that if you are gifted with the ability to help others heal, then you should share that gift with the world. He also mentioned that making money from sharing that gift was wrong and unethical. So this would mean that as an intuitive healer I am not meant to earn a living, but I am expected to sacrifice everything in order to share my gift with the world, because that is what is expected of me.

Spirit is not about sacrifice; ego is. I find it curious, because if an artist is gifted at painting, are they expected to share their gift with the world without any compensation? If someone is gifted at writing and singing music, are they expected to share their gift without getting paid to do it? We are all entitled to share our gift with the world and receive the abundance that comes from that genuine heart-led sharing. Can ego jump in here and derail us? Absolutely. Spiritual alignment does not guarantee financial abundance and the presence of financial abundance doesn't guarantee you are in alignment with Spirit. I have seen many spiritual teachers, as well as artists, musicians, business owners, counsellors, and corporate CEOs, who are not in alignment with Spirit despite making some really good money. I have also seen others who are in alignment with Spirit and who only make enough money to support their basic needs. And yes, there are also those who are in alignment and who are bathing in abundance while offering self-fulfilled service in the world.

> Spirit is not about sacrifice; ego is.

So which one do you want to be? Or which one are you currently being? Ghandi says "be the change you wish to see in the world". Are you in full alignment with your gift and sharing it authentically with the world to contribute to the healing of the planet? That is what we are all being called on to do right now. There is a sense of urgency and quickening in the awakening of our planet. The energy is rising and moving faster than ever before. Many of you already feel it. Those who are resisting it are experiencing great pain, because they are not aligning with the truth in their hearts. Remember, the greater the gap between what the mind thinks and what the heart knows, the greater the pain and suffering. Are you willing to align your head with your heart and follow your dreams? Are you willing to play big?

There is a call to your heart and the world needs you to answer. Your calling, whatever it may look like, will be a form of self-fulfilled service in the world. You may be called on to be a school janitor who inspires students to appreciate everything they have. You may be called on to speak on stage all around the world. You may be called on to open a daycare that fills the hearts of young children and teaches them to trust their intuition. You may be called to serve burgers with a loving smile that spreads to the heart of each and every customer. Whatever you are being called to do is an important role in the healing of our planet. There is no lead role. All parts contribute to the whole of its parts.

John Lesley—the son of my mentor Les Brown—once told me, "You can't fit a big-dream into a small life." At the time, I had my mind-body studio, I was supporting my Yoga for Fertility clients, I was already an author, and was teaching fitness and yoga instructors all around the world through my online instructor training programs. From the outside, it would appear my life was big, but in my heart I knew I was playing small. My life was small compared to the calling I had. The words that rang in my heart when I tuned into my calling were, "Speak to the world." I saw myself on a stage sharing a message from my heart with ten thousand strong in the audience. When I first saw this I was terrified, but the calling became stronger and stronger until I could no longer ignore it. It also became more painful because my heart's desire was a big dream and it didn't fit into the life I was living.

When I finally said "YES" to my calling, my life expanded, and within a year I closed my studio and launched my new speaking career. In August 2012, I spoke to an audience of ten thousand in Salt Lake City, Utah at the twentieth annual USANA Convention. My vision came to fruition when I shared my story about being an intuitive healer with the aim of inspiring others to stand up with courage and say, "This is who I am." I am deeply grateful for the opportunity and the miracles that allowed me to fulfill my life's purpose and heart's vision. The Universe is waiting for you to say "YES!". The miracles are all lined up for you as well, and the world is ready for your gift.

Are you playing small? As Marianne Williamson, another of my favourite authors, says, "Your playing small does not serve the world" (www.marianne.com). Keep in mind your "small" will look different from someone else's playing "small". Comparison is of the ego and will not serve you. You know in your heart if you are playing small, because when I pose the question you will feel a niggling or pain deep down inside. Only you will know if you are playing small or not. And only you can decide to let go of the life you think you want or need, to make room for the life you are meant to have.

♥ Heart Work: Being of Self-Fulfilled Service

Find stillness and take fifteen deep breaths in and out. Invite a state of peace and calm into your mind and body. Imagine your mind is wide open and drop your awareness into your heart. Ask your heart the following questions, and be curious about the first answers to pop into your mind.

1. What is my grandest dream?
2. What is my greatest desire?
3. What is my purpose in this world?
4. How am I meant to contribute to the healing of the planet?
5. What are some ways I can fill my heart and soul?
6. In what way can I use my talents and gifts to inspire global healing?

Chapter 6

Heart Led Living Principle ~ Be Open to Anything

We need to be willing to let go of anything we think we know and everything we think we don't know in order to be truly open to anything. Our ego would have us believe that we know what is best for ourselves, but we have no flipping clue. From our human perspective, we see limitations. The mind thinks it knows but our heart knows it knows. When we follow our heart and align with Spirit, we tap into an unlimited perspective. We need to be wide open and willing to let go in order for everything to unfold with perfection and grace. This requires an unwinding and emptying of our thinking mind so we make room for our inner wisdom to shine through and lead us on our heart's path. We let go of everything to be open to anything, which eventually leads to everything our heart desires.

> We let go of everything to be open to anything, which eventually leads to everything our heart desires.

What Would You Have Me Do Now?

When you become fully present to what is happening now, your life will expand and healing can occur. The secret to living a life with purpose and meaning is not out there somewhere. The answers you seek are not even in this book. The words and stories in this book are simply shining a light on the truth in your heart. The Sufi poet Rumi wrote, "What you seek is seeking you." The moment I stopped looking for happiness and love outside myself, and realized that it all comes from within me, everything changed. I discovered the secret to life is following my heart and trusting my intuition. My heart leads me to everything I seek and so much more. It all begins with learning to follow the signposts placed on your path by your intuitive heart and Spirit.

While I spent the first half of my life feeling like I was dying on the inside, there was something deep down inside that kept me going. Even in the darkest times, when I completely lost touch with the desire to live, a candle was burning in my heart and a soft voice of encouragement was speaking to me. It was the light of Spirit waiting with infinite patience for me to find my way back into my heart. Even though I didn't hear the voice in my heart, it was always there whispering love and guidance into my ear. It encouraged me back to the present moment, so I could remember the truth about myself. The more I looked outside myself for answers, the more signposts were placed on my path. If I missed one, another would show up.

The year 2001 was a powerful year of transformation and awakening for me. I entered the New Year seeking more and questioning the meaning of my life. I was yearning for internal happiness and peace. My desire for health and wholeness was growing, and I let go of the need to control. I shifted into a place of deep trust that something greater than myself was leading me on my path. All I needed to do was follow the signposts.

Transformation began when I woke up one morning, after a night of drinking, and had a sense that I needed to quit. The idea of never drinking again was terrifying, but I felt like my body was asking me to take a break. It was signpost number one, placed on my path by Spirit, leading me to stop drinking for thirty days. My ego quickly came on the scene, telling me I didn't want to miss out on anything, but I still decided I would stop drinking. However, I would continue to go out dancing with my friends.

Now let me take a moment to paint a picture here to help you understand just how significant this was. For the longest time, I was afraid to dance in front of anyone for fear of being judged. Up until this point, I would not dance unless I was drunk, or at least had a few drinks in me.

The first couple of weeks were tough, and the thought of having a drink was constantly on my mind. It was especially hard when all my friends were out together and everyone was drinking except me. I began to see the effects alcohol had on others, especially by the end of the night. I felt good waking up the next morning with a clear mind and feeling light in my body. I started to see how alcohol had negatively affected every area of my life, both physically and emotionally. I questioned whether I would ever drink again. When I look back now, I know I was successful, because the decision to quit for that period of time was completely heart-led. The guidance came directly from my heart, and my thoughts and beliefs were in full alignment with that choice.

I made it without a drop of alcohol and I learned to dance as if no one was watching. It was a huge accomplishment and I felt very proud of myself. Growing up, I had learned that you drink to get drunk. I really didn't know what a healthy relationship with alcohol was, but I was determined to try. After thirty days, I thought that I could introduce alcohol in again and that I would be able to create a healthy relationship with it. In the meantime, I didn't realize Spirit was leading me to let go of alcohol altogether, and it was my ego convincing me I could handle it now. I tried a few times and I couldn't have just one drink. The voice of my ego would come into my ear disguised as an encouraging voice, convincing me I could handle just one more. Our ego loves to take advantage of any weakness.

Spirit came in with signpost number two.

Around that same time, I decided to go out of town for the weekend with a group of friends. We drove about two hours outside Vancouver to Whistler, a popular ski village. That evening we all went out to a bar to have some drinks. I ordered a beer and took a sip. It didn't taste good at all. I thought it was because I had just come off a month of not drinking. It was like my taste buds had changed. Then, the reality hit me. I realized my menstrual cycle was late. The next day, I confirmed I was pregnant.

I immediately left Whistler without telling anyone and drove home. I was in shock but by the time I arrived home, I felt an excitement and a purpose I hadn't felt before. I was going to be a mother! Naturally, alcohol was the last thing on my mind, and it was easy to choose not to drink. After twelve weeks of celebrating my pregnancy and dreaming of motherhood, I experienced a miscarriage. It was one of the most devastating times of my life. After two surgeries, antibiotics to treat an infection, intense physical and emotional pain, I crawled out of isolation with a deep desire to be a mother. Thoughts of drinking again crept into my mind. It was my ego convincing me it was the best way to deal with the pain.

I decided I would visit my family in Ontario as I recovered and healed from my miscarriage. I spent some time with my Dad and during that time I noticed that his energy was quite low; I could see the light in his eyes was dim. My father never really talked about his health and he didn't seem interested in sharing anything with me during that visit. I let it go, even though I had a sense he was quite ill.

Along came Spiritual signpost number three.

In July, three months later, I received a phone call that my Dad had severe liver damage and needed a liver transplant. I knew in my heart that it was worse than everyone was letting on. Within a few weeks, his second wife called to say my Dad was in the hospital, that he had three to six months to live, and that he did not qualify for a liver transplant. I immediately booked a flight.

When I first walked into the hospital room, I saw such pain in his eyes. His body was weak and his skin was jaundiced from liver failure. I hugged him and gave him a kiss. I told him I would be there as long as he needed me to be. All my commitments fell away, and I knew in my heart this was where I needed to be. Fear of finances, clients, and everything else that used to seem so important, all dropped away. I was fully present and grateful to be with my father.

On day four, we knew he was getting worse and that it was

just a matter of time before he would pass away. The doctor's timeline of three to six months became three to six days. His body was giving up. Every time he moved, I saw pain in his eyes, and my sister and I decided to speak with the nurse. They were willing to give him something for the pain, but they told us that his liver wouldn't be able to process it effectively. We both knew in our hearts that it was better for him to be relieved of the pain. We made that choice for him.

The next day, he was unable to get up or speak. All he could do was wiggle his nose to acknowledge our presence. I felt the love coming from his heart and, at the same time, I was aware of his fear. As his condition quickly worsened, my sister and I slept overnight on cots beside his bed and took turns staying up to watch him rest. I would whisper into his ear that he was strong and courageous. I told him that he didn't have to be afraid. There was great love for him here on Earth, but there was also great love waiting for him as he made his transition back to Spirit.

> I told him that he didn't have to be afraid. There was great love for him here on Earth, but there was also great love waiting for him as he made his transition back to Spirit.

On day five, he was fully unconscious. In the afternoon, as the sun streamed through the window, I was sitting by his side stroking his hair and my brother was sitting nearby. I was surprised by how soft my Dad's hair was. He always had that "Elvis slick hair" look, which I assumed would either be hard as a rock or greasy to touch.

I looked at my brother and asked, "Do you think he knows it's okay to go?"

My brother responded, "I don't know, but I don't want to be here."

I replied, "That's okay. I will be here."

I sent a heart message to my Dad saying, "It's okay to let go." I told him I loved him and that I will miss him, but that he didn't have to hang on any longer.

A few minutes later, my grandfather came in the room and asked my brother to come with him to move the car. My brother left the room. My Dad's wife, my grandmother, and my sister all came back into the room and gathered around his bed. We all watched in silence as he took his last breath. Tears of relief came down my face and I could sense he was finally at peace.

As I walked out of the hospital, a clear message came into my heart: I made the choice to stop drinking as a way to honour my father. I had watched my father struggle with alcohol for as long as I can remember. In fact, I saw how I was repeating many of those patterns in my own relationship with alcohol. I didn't want his death to be in vain, void of meaning. I realized he had died very young and that there was so much more he could have shared. It was in that moment I realized I had a reason to live. I refused to die with my music still in me. I was going to do everything possible to turn my life around and follow my heart's calling to be of service to others. It was time to shine my light! I became determined to shine it as brightly as I possibly can, and in order to do that I needed to let go of alcohol.

I walked my father to the edge of life and gave him permission to leave, and at the same time, I gave myself permission to live!

Signpost number four around alcohol came in 2009 when my liver caused my skin to become jaundiced, much like my father's had in his last days. While I had already quit drinking, the thought of drinking still came into my mind occasionally. I would never act on those thoughts, but they were there, lurking alongside my ego.

When I returned from Sanoviv in 2011 and after healing cancer in my body, it became a spiritual knowing in my heart that alcohol was never going to be a part of my life again. It became crystal clear that alcohol was an ego distraction that would keep me from embracing my gift as an intuitive. It not only lowered my vibration; it would also block my intuitive gifts.

Allow me to take a moment to explain vibration here. Everything in this world vibrates. Even things that seem stationary from our human perspective are actually moving. This is all governed by the Law of Vibration. Everything has a calibrated rate of vibration including thoughts, emotions, food, alcohol, etc. That calibration will either be creative or destructive. This calibration influences the secondary law, which is the Law of Attraction, which many people became aware of from the movie, *The Secret*. Most people believe that the Law of Attraction is how they manifest certain circumstances in their life, but actually the Law of Vibration is primarily responsible. That is why you will not manifest something you want to attract—even if you are thinking about it over and over again in your mind—unless you feel it deep in your heart. If there is something you wish to attract into your life, you must become a vibrational match for it. If you are not in vibrational alignment with it, you will not attract it. So for me alcohol and the effects of drinking lowered my vibration and became physically and emotionally destructive. It also lowered my vibration to a level that blocked my intuitive gift as a healer.

In order to be fully aligned with Spirit, I need to be fully present and aware of life as it unfolds in each moment. My intuitive abilities continue to get stronger every day. I am helping more and more people now, as I have been able to transition from helping one client at a time to facilitating group healings in audiences of any size.

For me, following my heart and paying attention to the signposts are not just part of my core message: they are a way of life. In every moment, I tune into my inner guide and ask, "What would you have me do now?" I follow my heart no matter what.

You also have an internal GPS that is ready to lead you in every moment. When you were born you trusted your intuition, but somewhere along the way you were taught to disconnect from it. As you learn to tune in and trust it again, you will discover a sense of peace, ease, and grace. As you follow the spiritual signposts and go with the flow, attachment to pain and suffering will fall away. It sounds simple, but it is not always easy. That is why I created our *Heart Led Living* community, so we can join together and support each other in order to unwind the ego mindset, trust our intuition, and heal.

Here is a comment around the process of unwinding from one of my *Heart Led Living* members Kelly Van Unen: "It's a funny thing; we come into this life and we take years to learn things and then we come to realize that much of what we have learned we must undo in order to be our authentic self."

I choose to see life's challenges, including death, as opportunities to heal, grow, and step into our light. I have learned to be open to signposts and I am able to learn the lessons quickly, without as much pain. Are you willing to watch for signposts so you can awaken your full potential now?

Are you willing to release any and all attachments so you can be fully open to the guidance as it comes in each moment? We are all here for a reason. My life matters and so does yours! Yes. Your life matters! You have a unique gift that you are meant to share with the world. Those that are meant to hear your voice are waiting for your gift. As you become fully present to each moment, you will be led toward sharing your gift in the most powerful way.

> You have a unique gift that you are meant to share with the world.

♥ Heart Work: What Would You Have Me Do Now?

"What would you have me do now?" is one of the most powerful open-ended questions I ask Spirit. The answers that come into my awareness often surprise me. When you stop and become fully present, you open your heart and mind to receive guidance. You let go of what you think you should do, and tap into the place within you that knows what you are meant to do.

Whatever You Go Through, You Grow Through

Are you afraid of the unknown? Are you comfortable with change? There are so many people who choose to play it safe or repeat the same routine day in and day out, because they are afraid of change. When we look at nature we can quickly find evidence that change is inevitable.

Dr. Christiane Northrup has taught me that we either grow or we die trying not to. Change is happening whether we want it to or not. We are growing in every moment, whether we are aware of it or not. There are definitely some people growing at a faster rate than others, but everyone is growing and everything is constantly changing. When we learn to come into a place of acceptance and surrender around change, we will find peace. When we resist change, we resist life. When we resist life, life appears to resist us.

I had a client who was in a relationship that was no longer healthy. Neither she nor her husband was happy. Over the period of a year, in numerous private yoga therapy sessions, her relationship would come up. She knew in her heart that she needed to leave the relationship, but the fear of leaving was stronger than her desire to follow her intuition. I held a space of non-judgment and encouragement, as she would find excuse after excuse of why it wasn't the right time to leave. Finally, one day she came in and shared that her marriage was over and that she had had the "sweaty palm conversation". Through that experience, she realized how painful it was to remain static and at the same time, she recognized it was all purposeful. She learned that following her intuition was important, and taking inspired action in spite of fear was vital in order for her to stay in a place of peace. Change is not always easy, but it is necessary. We can either resist it or embrace it.

I see every moment as an opportunity to heal and grow.

Whether you are releasing a past trauma by bringing your awareness to a present-moment trigger, or practising mindfulness with Spirit, every moment is a gift and an opportunity to heal. Yes, challenging occurrences happen, but you can learn to process and integrate the experience by being fully present to every situation as it unfolds. Full present-moment awareness allows you to grow through situations as they occur. This ensures that you don't carry the burdens or baggage of the past with you any longer. Remember, we heal the past in the present moment, by processing triggers as they occur here and now.

> We heal the past in the present moment, by processing triggers as they occur here and now.

Be open and willing to look at the upset in the moment. That is where healing occurs. You don't heal your past by going back into it. You heal and make peace with past trauma by processing the emotions, thoughts, and beliefs that are affecting you in this moment. Spirit works in the present moment only. Your internal guidance system is ready to help you heal any upset, no matter how big or small. When I look back at my life experiences, I am often surprised by how much I endured and how strong I am today due to everything I lived through. Your past does not define you, but the experiences have shaped you.

The book *A Course in Miracles*, scribed by Helen Schucman, Ph.D. and William Thetford, Ph.D., teaches that "you are never upset for the reason you think". Anytime I am upset, feel uneasy, or worried, I immediately examine what I am experiencing. I am wide open to any insight. I am uncompromising with my commitment to heal. Over the years, I have also become much more sensitive to pain and resistance, and can no longer tolerate it for longer than a few hours.

When I first opened my mind-body studio, I had let go of everything else, all my fitness classes, kickboxing clients, and my position at a local health club as a group fitness coordinator. I was guided to focus all my energy and time on my own studio.

As I unwound from everything that had kept me so busy for so long, I started to feel anger and frustration rising to the surface. I started to yell at my kids and my dogs when they weren't listening. Of course, after yelling I would feel guilty, because I wasn't being a patient-enough mother. It continued for about two weeks and I could feel this volcano of rage bubbling deep inside me.

In spite of all the tools I had, I couldn't get to the root of my anger on my own. I needed help and I needed it right away. My mentor Les Brown always tells me, "Ask for help, not because you are weak but because you want to remain strong." I have learned to ask for help without self-judgment. Initially, I tried getting an appointment with a counsellor, but she was out of town and unavailable. The Universe made sure that door was closed so I would look elsewhere. After searching online, I found a local psychotherapist who also integrated yoga therapy into her practice. It was divine synchronicity; when I called, she just happened to have a cancellation that day that fit perfectly into my schedule.

During the session, I shared about my outbursts of anger and feelings of rage bubbling up. It was all focused on triggers when my children weren't listening or when the dogs didn't listen. As I shared my story, she held me in a yoga posture to help facilitate the release of the trigger in my physical body. I could feel a deep sense of fear, and memories of being sexually abused when I was five-years-old came into my awareness. I felt uncomfortably vulnerable as tears rolled down my face and my body shook with deep fear. The fear felt life-threatening and the safety of my children filled my entire being. The words "When you don't listen, bad things happen" began ringing in my ears, and I felt a deep sense of panic wash over me as vivid images of that childhood trauma flashed through my mind. I began repeating the words "I am safe. I am safe. I am safe", and my body suddenly stopped shaking and peace filled my heart.

I realized that I wasn't angry with my children or my dogs for not listening. My deep-seated fear was related to a childhood trauma and the blame I held toward myself, because I didn't listen and something bad happened. My fear showed up as anger in the present moment, when someone wasn't listening: I was the one who hadn't listened as a child. It was intense "life or death" fears that led me to blow up with anger. It was anger underscored by underlying panic that something bad was going to happen if they didn't listen to me.

After that session, I was much more patient with my children and my dogs, and curiously they began to listen again. The Universe provides the life experiences we need in order to heal anything we are holding that no longer serves our highest good. I had done a lot of healing around that childhood trauma already, but it was time for me to heal that layer of fear. Once I let it go and healed deep in my body, I finally felt the peace of mind and the deep trust that I am safe and all is well.

Whatever you are going through, you can grow through, as long as you practise present-moment awareness. Be curious without judgment. Be open to a new perspective. Allow your heart to lead you to those who can support you, or to the book or audio program that will help bring clarity around a life challenge. Every moment is an opportunity to heal. Every obstacle is an opportunity in disguise. Everything happens for a reason and it is all for our highest good. As we heal our hearts, we contribute to global healing. Be willing to grow through life and your experience of life's challenges will be transformed right before your eyes.

♥ Heart Work: You Are Never Upset for the Reason You Think

The next time you have negative emotions that surface, be willing to consider that you are not upset for the reason you think, just as *A Course in Miracles* advises us. The present moment trigger is designed to bring buried emotions to the surface for healing. It is an opportunity to heal the past in the present.

Find stillness and silence. Take eight deep breaths and ask Spirit to show you the root of the upset. Take your time and be willing and open to explore all five bodies: physical, mental, emotional, energetic, and spiritual. When you recognize that the negative emotion is not always about what is happening, but rather about what happened in your past, you allow compassion for self and anyone else involved to enter in. Once you have the awareness around the reasons for your upset, the FEAR process in Chapter Three can also be helpful to clear the fear away.

Raising the Roof

We all have internal set points for what we allow ourselves to feel and experience in this life. These "upper limits"—as New York Times best-selling author and psychologist Dr. Gay Hendricks refers to them in his book *The Big Leap* (published by HarperOne in 2010)—are determined at a very young age. To understand what these internal set points or upper limits are, consider that a thermostat set very low keeps the temperature of the room cold. If the temperature rises, the cold air turns on automatically to maintain a specific set point. The temperature doesn't really get a chance to go over a certain level, because the thermostat controls it. We have internal set points for everything: love, joy, pleasure, abundance, and happiness. These set points were established when we were very young and they influence all our decisions at a deep subconscious level. If we reach the upper limit, it can feel overwhelming and self-sabotage kicks in to bring us back down to our set point.

> We have internal set points for everything: love, joy, pleasure, abundance, and happiness.

Dr. Hendricks explains all the common upper limit problems in The Big Leap . His many insightful gems changed my life in many powerful ways. The biggest gem I learned was how to identify my upper-limit problems and self-sabotaging behaviours.

I have many examples I can share here, because I had very

low set points for most "feel-good" emotions. I will share two that were the most purposeful. My set point for abundance was set very low as a child. I watched my mother struggle to raise three kids on her own, with very little to no financial support. I became accustomed to living from paycheque to paycheque, and, more often, from less than paycheque to paycheque. I learned to work hard with strong work ethics, yet to stay in the familiar set point of living paycheque to paycheque. My set point for financial abundance was low. If I suddenly received money above and beyond my regular cheque, I would find something to spend it on. I was actually responsible with my spending and would invest it wisely, but I never chose to put in the bank for savings. That would have raised my set point; it was uncomfortable for me because it was unfamiliar. Spending money in this example may not sound like self-sabotage, but it was, because it kept me from really living fully. It kept me from achieving my dream of owning a property with a goat and a horse. I will share a little later how I raised the roof on my abundance set point, but I would like to share another example first.

My set points for happiness and joy were also set very low from childhood. For example, if the highest set point for joy is ten, mine was around three. My happiness set point was set around five. Anytime I experienced joy or happiness above my familiar set points I would feel overwhelmed and do something to self-sabotage them. That way I could return to the lower set point that felt more comfortable, because it was what I was used to.

When I would go beyond my set point for happiness, I would feel overwhelmed to the point where I could barely breathe. My self-sabotaging behaviour would kick in and I would start to criticize. I would go from feeling happy and excited about something one minute to find myself criticizing others on the road and feeling annoyed and frustrated the next minute. Or I would start to nitpick at my husband and criticize him. I would start to feel bad and my happiness setting would lower back into my familiar zone, and the overwhelm would dissipate.

I became determined to overcome this self-sabotaging behaviour, so I told my husband about my pattern of becoming critical. He started to call me out on it as soon as I started to nitpick. My first response would be my ego jumping in with disappointment, because I was exposed, "Crap! Why did I tell him about this? Now I have awareness and have to do something about it." My second response was, "Thank you for reminding me!" and I would start my process of "raising the roof".

"Raising the roof" is something that has worked not only for me but also my clients, when they would reach a familiar threshold or set point. The same way in which you can increase the temperature set point on a thermostat, you can raise the set point on your personal upper limits as well. I began to set the intention to "raise the roof" of my set point. When I felt overwhelmed, it was almost a claustrophobic feeling, like the walls or ceiling were closing in on me. I would imagine putting my hands above my head and pushing the roof up slightly. Sometimes, it moved a millimetre, and other times it would move a few inches. I would celebrate the fact that it had moved and make a conscious choice to increase my internal set point forever.

♥ Heart Work: Raising the Roof

Now it is your turn to explore your internal set points and raise your roof. It all begins with increasing your awareness of your self-sabotaging behaviours. Here is a list of behaviours and emotions to watch for.

1. Worry – this is the quickest and most effective way to self-sabotage. The ego loves the energy of worry and can easily take you down into a wormhole and hold you in a pattern of non-action through worry.
2. Blame – whether we start blaming ourself or someone else, blame is a holding pattern that will keep us from exploring the true upset.

3. Procrastination – this is doing everything else but what we know we are guided to do. We are putting off the inevitable whether it is feeling what we need to feel or completing a task that needs to be done.

4. Quitting – wanting to quit is often accompanied with feelings of overwhelm. I have had days where I will call up my friend Lisa and tell her I quit everything, including my life, and I am going to move to Africa and live in a hut.

5. Avoidance – denying or hiding feelings and/or avoiding people or situations.

6. Paralyzed – this is where we feel like we are stopped dead in our tracks with fear.

7. Masking – many people use food, alcohol, and other substances and behaviours to numb out or mask how they are feeling.

These are the most common ones I have come across. I strongly recommend you read the book *The Big Leap* to learn more upper limit behaviours. The more awareness you have, the better equipped you will be to raise your roof and transform your self-sabotaging behaviours.

Once you identify your most common upper limits, begin to make a conscious effort to stop the behaviours in the moment you are aware of them. This is similar to how I asked my husband to call me out on my behaviour while I was doing it. This way you can make a choice to "raise the roof." Be sure to release any judgment when you have the awareness. Your ego is trying to convince you that you failed once again and that you should know better. Be wide open and remain curious without judgment, and the moment you have awareness, practise acceptance. Your dialogue might go something like this: "I am blaming and it's okay. It is what it is, and it's okay. At least now, I have the ability to raise the roof." You might even be inspired to dance around and raise your hands in the air as you "raise the roof". It is your roof and you can raise it in whatever way feels good for you. Have fun with it. Get excited about it. Be patient, persistent, and determined to heal. When you align with Spirit, there is no limit to the love, joy, happiness, and abundance you will experience. Be open to anything.

The Day I Fired My Ego

Marianne Williamson shared on Facebook, "Enlightenment is not learning a new thought system; it's the process of unlearning a thought system that the world has taught you." If you want to align fully with your heart's path and life's purpose, you need to align fully with your inner guide. You will need to go through a process of unwinding, which is an unlearning of all the thoughts, beliefs, and rules you learned throughout your life. You need to be willing to give up everything you think you know in your mind, so you can tap into the deep knowing in your heart. Unwinding is also a process of releasing anything and everything that is being held in any of the five bodies: physical, mental, emotional, energetic, and spiritual.

One day, I woke up inspired to create a new audio program for my business. During my meditation, I was shown the title and format. I was inspired to create a PowerPoint presentation with beautiful vibrant photos. It all came together, and easily. I was in the creative flow and fully aligned with Spirit. Once I had completed the PowerPoint, I wanted to start recording the audio for the program so I could launch it the following week. That is when everything started to feel like an effort. I would start recording, and suddenly the program would close. I would open it up only to find what I had recorded so far had not saved. So I started again. I felt like I was forcing the words and it didn't feel authentic. It wasn't flowing; it was forcing, and it didn't feel good. I kept going for another half hour and suddenly tuned into the pain in my back. It had gotten so loud I couldn't ignore it any longer, so I stopped recording and went to my yoga mat to stretch out my back. Once I found stillness, I realized I was choosing ego as my teacher. When I reflected a little deeper, I discovered that ego was actually acting as my boss and was aiming for complete control of my business. That was the day I chose to fire my ego. I declared out loud, "You are not the boss of me or my business", and I imagined firing him, asking ego to leave the building.

I took over and decided I would run my business my way. After all, I had twenty years of experience being an entrepreneur. I started back into my recording and still felt some resistance, so I put the project aside until I had more clarity and creative flow. The next few days it was still left to the side. It started to niggle at me as an incomplete task. Weeks went by and I was constantly wondering when I would be inspired to complete it. I started to release any and all fearful thoughts the moment they entered my mind. I started challenging any thought or belief that was not in alignment with my heart's knowing. I would wait for clarity and take inspired action only. I was doing less, but being more. I was being guided through a process of unwinding everything I thought I knew, or didn't know, about running my own business. The truth is that once I fired my ego, I had no idea what needed to be done. Then I remembered that I am either in alignment with ego or Spirit.

> Doing less and being more.

I had fired my ego, but had never consciously hired Spirit. Spirit was waiting with infinite patience for me to surrender my business and let Spirit take the lead. Now Spirit is my boss and ego has no role in my business; I am simply the vessel, the same way I am a vessel for the words in this book to flow through me. I have surrendered my business and my life to Spirit, so that my heart can lead me to the path I am meant to be on. Shortly after that shift, I was guided back to the recording and completed it within three hours. The words flowed perfectly and easily as I allowed Spirit to speak through me.

The process of unlearning and unwinding can be challenging,

but it is necessary. I encourage you to surrender your business, your health, your relationships, your finances, and essentially your entire life, to Spirit. Start with one area and begin to unwind. When we unwind from everything we think we know, we become wildly open to everything we are meant to know. Embrace the idea that you have no idea. Get out of your head and let your heart lead the way. You will be surprised where it leads you. Remember, when you get insight or have a vision of something, your ego will want to fill in the gap with a big story or the most amazing plan. Stay tuned in and allow your heart to lead you in each moment. Watch for signs of resistance showing up as technological challenges, interruptions, lack of creativity, worry, fear, or forcing. If there is nothing you are clearly guided to do, then there is nothing to do. Spirit can only communicate with us when we are fully present to this moment. Another important point is that when it comes to surrender, Spirit works on a need-to-know basis. You will be shown what you need to see in divine timing. Spirit will give you a glimpse of something on your path, only if it is purposeful.

> Spirit works on a need-to-know basis.

♥ Heart Work: Fire Your Ego

Make a conscious choice to fire your ego. Thank your ego for all he has done and let him know he is no longer in charge. Then make a conscious choice to hire Spirit as your boss and surrender your issue. Be open and willing to follow your intuition and make choices from a place of love, clarity, and purpose. When you do, you will become so much more efficient. You will get way more done in less time and feel much more fulfilled with your work. I even tune in for guidance around reading emails. I am guided when to open emails to read them and I am also guided when to delete them. Sometimes I am shown to delete an email without ever reading it. Your level of trust will increase over time. I have learned to trust that Spirit is working for me and I am completely taken care of. I receive directions and I follow. Remember, the process of unwinding may take some time. Be patient and practise self-compassion. Let go of the need to control; trust that all is well and all will be well.

I am Wildly Open to Receive

What does it take to be wildly open to receive? To what extent are you open to receive abundance, love, joy, or pleasure? In Heart Led Living, we teach to be open to anything and attached to nothing. Being wildly open means we are open to anything that is on our heart's path. We are open to receive love with our whole heart. We are open to experience joy. We are open to enjoy financial abundance in our life. So, if we could experience such a vibrant life by being wildly open, why do so many people have trouble receiving?

Take a moment to explore your ability to give and receive. Which do you find easier? I speak about this in several areas of my book, because it is an essential piece in the healing process. Most people, especially women, are natural givers. We are natural nurturers. We are not natural receivers.

The main reason people are not open to receive is rooted in a feeling of unworthiness. It will show up in a variety of different ways. Our ego loves to play the unworthiness card. People don't feel comfortable being happy when others in the world are suffering. They may feel guilty for having financial abundance when others are living without food and shelter. They may feel sorry for others and/or feel like they don't want to make others feel badly for what they don't have. This leads to feelings of shame and guilt for having all that they have, and those emotions will block everything that is meant to come to them.

At one point when I was running my mind-body studio, I realized I was playing the "Even Steven" game with my finances. I would have a good income one month and invest more money into something new for the studio the next month. I saw this pattern play out for a while before I clued in to the fact that I was open to the studio earning more money, but I wasn't open to having enough left over to pay myself. After going into meditation and self-reflection, I realized I was carrying guilt right between my shoulder blades. This area is the back of the heart chakra (energy centre), our most common area to receive. Guilt was blocking it. As I looked a little deeper, I felt an issue surface: a fear of outshining my mother. I was afraid to earn more money than her, because I didn't want her to feel badly. The words of Marianne Williamson rang through my mind,

"There is nothing enlightened about shrinking so that other people won't feel insecure around you. We are all meant to shine, as children do. We were born to make manifest the glory of God that is within us. It's not just in some of us; it's in everyone. And as we let our own light shine, we unconsciously give other people permission to do the same. As we are liberated from our own fear, our presence automatically liberates others."

I felt a deep shift and I was able to release the guilt and give it over to Spirit for healing at the deepest possible level.

The other common block I see is around love. Many of my clients have used a shield of armour around their heart to keep them from being hurt. While at some point in their life, the shield protected them, at another point it starts harming them. It actually causes more hurt, because they are blocking out the love that they deserve. The old saying, "Love as if you have never been hurt", is so true. The truth is no one can hurt you: you are the only one who can choose to feel hurt by what another person does. It is your choice to feel or carry hurt. That perspective allows you to stand in your power and hold your light no matter what comes your way. Are you willing to open your heart to receive love? Are you committed to heal your past so you can experience life fully and feel all the love, joy, happiness, and abundance that is your birthright?

> No one can hurt you: you are the only one who can
> choose to feel hurt by what another person does.

Here is a poem I wrote after my miscarriage in 2001. I also read these words at my father's funeral. I often re-read them as a reminder to choose life and be open to receive love. I hope "Trust in Love" inspires you.

Trust in Love
by Sue Dumais

People come in and out of our lives every day.
Some impact our lives more than others.
There are those who touch us so powerfully
that we will never be the same again.
We need to cherish those experiences and
appreciate the lessons in our lives.
Each experience is an opportunity to be human.
Each lesson is a step to becoming more aware.
It is human to feel pain, fear, and guilt.
It is also human to feel love.
It is a shame to see the walls of protection
surrounding each of us.
They are only shielding out the love we all deserve.
Being open to experience is being willing to feel;
To feel fear, to feel pain, and more importantly to feel love.
Trust in the experiences of your life
And you shall bathe in the love that surrounds you.

♥ Heart Work: I am Wildly Open to Receive

Stand tall and feel a connection with the earth beneath your feet. Take ten deep falling-out breaths. A falling-out breath is where you inhale through the nose and exhale through the mouth with a sigh. Raise your arms out to the side and open your heart. Set an intention to release and heal any and all hurts, pain, and suffering that prevent you from being fully open to receive. If there is something specific you would like to open up your heart to, then be specific. For example, if you wish to be wildly open to receive love or abundance, use those specific words in your declaration. Below is a sample declaration you can use to craft your own. The declaration needs to resonate deep in your heart and soul. Many times when you find your words of declaration, they resonate so deeply in your heart that you will feel emotional. That is good. Allow the expression of any and all emotions and keep repeating the words.

Love Declaration:

"I am wildly open to receive love with my whole heart. I choose to release and heal anything that is not in alignment with this declaration. I give all thoughts, beliefs, and emotions over to Spirit and I ask for healing on the deepest possible level. I am wildly open to receive love with my whole heart. I am deeply grateful for the love I already feel in my heart and I am open to experience even greater levels. Thank you! Thank you! Thank you!"

Abundance Declaration:

"I am wildly open to receive financial abundance with my whole heart. I choose to release and heal anything that is not in alignment with this declaration. I give all thoughts, beliefs, and emotions over to Spirit and I ask for healing on the deepest possible level. I am wildly open to receive financial abundance with my whole heart. I am deeply grateful for money I already have and I am open to receive even greater amounts. I make a conscious choice to withdraw from my spiritual bank and make a generous deposit into my earth bank. I do so with deep gratitude in my heart. Thank you! Thank you! Thank you!"

Chapter 7

Heart Led Living Principle ~ Be Curious

Curiosity is a powerful tool that instantly dissolves judgment. It completely opens our mind to new possibilities and unlimited potential. A curious mind is a healthy mind awaiting guidance from the heart. In *Heart Led Living*, we practise being curious, because the truth is we have no clue how to do this thing called life. We like to think we know, but we have absolutely no clue. The good news is, our heart knows. Spirit knows. When we choose to align with curiosity, we are choosing to be wide open to receive guidance. When we are willing to release the need to know, we can drop into a deep place of trust and know that the answer will come with divine timing. Being curious frees us from judgment and allows us to be open to find meaning in the present moment. In other words, a curious mind is a peaceful mind.

> Curiosity is a powerful tool that instantly dissolves judgment. A curious mind is a peaceful mind.

I Don't Know, But I'm Curious

The biggest block in the mind is that we think we know what we don't know. The ego loves when we question things, especially when we question from a place of fear. We are taught to fear the unknown. The problem is that everything is unknown, so we end up living in fear about everything. We have no idea what is going to happen. We think we have control, but we don't. Our ego wants to keep us trying to control that which is uncontrollable, because when we do this, we feel more and more out of control.

We have two options: we are either in a space of trying to control or we are in a mindset of trust. Trust and control cannot exist at the same time. Control is based on fear and is of the ego; trust is based on love and is in alignment with Spirit. The choice is yours in each moment. Will you trust or control?

> Trust and control cannot exist at the same time.

I remember that as a child I always needed to know where we were going, how long it would take, and who would be there. I was always nervous and anxious. Although I was good at hiding my true feelings so that I wouldn't be a burden to others, inside me there was a constant storm of worry and fear. I have memories of watching my mother struggle with money, time, and energy. My Mom always did the best she could to provide a good home for us. She was a hard-working, single mom doing everything she could to be there for us. She was always working long hours, just to make ends meet. We struggled financially, and I could see and feel how hard, emotional, and worrying the situation was for my Mom.

As a child, my ego began to feed thoughts into my mind. "If I wasn't born, maybe my parents would have stayed together. If I wasn't born, maybe my Mom would be able to take more time to rest and less time to worry. If I wasn't born, maybe my brother and sister would have a better life. If I wasn't born, I wouldn't be such a burden to everyone."

I want to be clear: my mother never ever gave me reason to believe I was a burden. She was loving, supportive, and sacrificed a lot for us. It was my ego that made me believe I was a burden. This belief began to filter into every area of my life and I spent most of my childhood trying to make up for my sense of unworthiness. At the time I couldn't control the fact that I thought I was a burden; but I could do my best to be as invisible as possible or to help out as much as I could to help lift the burden I placed on others by being alive. At a very deep level, this belief has driven me to be of service to others. I wanted to help save the world in an attempt to save myself and prove my worthiness.

It was not until after my son was born that I had the awareness of carrying the burden of being born. In the first three months of my son's life, I was amazed and in love with his innocence. It was such a sacred time, and although it was extremely challenging and I got very little sleep, I was so grateful for this precious gift. One time when speaking to my Mom, I asked her about my birth. We had never talked about my birth before, and up until that point I had never asked. It was extremely therapeutic for me. I realized the belief that I had been a burden had been wrong all along.

One day, tears began to fill my eyes while watching my son sleep in my arms, and I realized that I too was born innocent and precious. Suddenly, he opened his eyes and stared deep into my eyes with such love. It was the first time, other than with my husband, that I had felt like someone really saw the real me, and I felt so much love it was overwhelming at first. My heart expanded that day into the truth that my life is purposeful and that I am loved as long as I am open to receive love from others. I had no idea what my son would bring to my life. I still don't have a clue about the whole picture, but I do know that he was well worth the wait.

When my husband and I first started trying to conceive a child, I thought I had it all figured out. After all, you go your entire life trying not to get pregnant, so when you start trying to conceive, you feel it should happen right away. It took two years to conceive my son. It was a monthly, emotional roller coaster of ups and downs, anticipation and disappointment, excitement and loss. Every month felt like a year had passed. Eventually, I came to a place of acceptance: "I don't know when it will happen and it's okay." Someone reminded me that a baby also decides when to come into this world. It wasn't just up to me or my husband. I surrendered even more to the concept of "I don't know; I have no clue, and worrying is not helping".

Today, I look at life as an adventure. I never really know what's going to happen and that's exciting! In *Heart Led Living*, we constantly repeat, "I don't know, but I'm curious." You have no way of predicting what may or may not happen in the future, so there's no point in worrying about it.

> "Worrying is using your imagination to create something you don't want." Abraham-Hicks, inspirational speaker.

Heart Led Living's "I don't know and it's okay" evolved into a second step "I don't know, but I'm curious". I became open to alternative therapies and different approaches to natural conception. I began to follow my heart and remain curious about where it would lead me on my own fertility journey. Curiosity eliminated judgment. Having a curious mindset without the need to know also helped when I opened my studio and started teaching Yoga for Fertility Classes, running support groups, and supporting women and couples in conceiving their dreams. I could never have predicted the gifts my fertility journey would bring to my life, as well as to the lives of countless couples all around the world.

Looking back at my fertility journey, I'm glad I didn't know how it was going to play out. I needed to go through everything I did, so I could learn to mother myself before my son arrived. I am a better mother because of it. My fertility journey became a path to my spiritual awakening, full of powerful lessons and deep healing for me and many others. My relationship with my husband is stronger for it. My love and appreciation for life is greater and I have deep compassion for others on their path to conception. I have gained such deep trust in my intuition that I was able to let go of our dream of having another child with peace and certainty. In our hearts, our family is complete with our son and daughter, and all of our critters, of course. I have come to a place of peace and gratitude. "I don't know, but I am curious" recently became "I don't know and I am glad". I can fully embrace the adventure of life without needing to know, and with deep gratitude for the unknown.

Are you willing to trust that everything is playing out exactly as it needs to for your highest good and healing? Every situation, interaction and experience is designed to awaken you to your calling. Every challenge is shining light on an area of your life that you still need to heal. When you judge what is happening, you are choosing the ego as your teacher. The ego loves judgment. It feeds and thrives on it.

When you practise curiosity, there is no room for judgment in your mind. When you add curiosity to acceptance, you have the perfect recipe for healing and spiritual alignment. Adopt the motto of "I don't know and it's okay; I don't know but I'm curious". When you stop judging why something is happening, you become open to receive insight about what to do. Curiosity allows you to see the situation from a new perspective.

> When you add curiosity to acceptance, you have the perfect recipe for healing and spiritual alignment.

This is where the practice of hindsight enters the scene. I am sure you can look back at your life and remember a challenging time. As you look back from this moment, using hindsight, you can see the gifts or lessons that came from it and how it contributed to who you are today. What if you could practise "present-moment hindsight"? With a curious mind, you can be open to the gift, lesson, or insight as you are actually going through the experience or challenge. In many situations, this skill allows me to find meaning while I am still in the midst of the perceived chaos. In finding meaning, I find peace, and in the peace I return back into alignment with Spirit as my teacher.

You can receive guidance from Spirit in each moment to lead you through the darkness and back into the light. A curious mind is a gift, and it will free you to be fully present to each moment as it unfolds.

♥ Heart Work: I Don't Know

Step One:

"I don't know and it's okay." This allows you to make peace with "what is". It removes ego's judgments and allows you to let go of what or where you thought you should be. Acceptance of "what is" allows for a powerful shift from ego back into alignment with Spirit.

Step Two:

"I don't know, but I'm curious." When you move from acceptance into surrender, you shift from the need to control the uncontrollable to trust that all is well and all will be well. The moment you surrender everything you think you know, you will tap into the place deep within that knows without thinking. You are being held in love and guided by Spirit. You are so taken care of.

The moment you surrender everything you think you know, you will tap into the place deep within that knows without thinking.

Step Three:

"I don't know and I'm glad." As you accept and surrender in a deep place of trust, you become excited about the adventure that is your life. Every moment becomes a gift that you unwrap with anticipation and appreciation. Life is happening for you, and everything is playing out for your highest good and the good of those around you.

Unwinding, Undoing, and Understanding

Our ego jumps at any chance it sees to take charge of our minds and control our lives. Our ego begins to infiltrate our mind at a very young age and, over time, we learn by example that ego is the boss. We slowly lose connection with Spirit and begin to distrust our own internal guidance system. We lose touch with our intuition and conform to society's ego-driven mindset. The good news is that it is never too late to re-align with our inner guide. The more people who remember the truth and re-align with Spirit as their guide, the more we contribute to the healing of our planet. Collectively, we can change society's ego-driven rules. We must first begin with our own unwinding process.

When I first began to unwind my mind, it was like trying to unravel a gigantic ball of yarn. In the beginning, it didn't seem to be doing anything but bringing up all the suffering from my past. My thoughts were intense and cruel, providing a constant storm. When I started counselling for my eating disorder, I was trying to heal my body, mind, and spirit through talk therapy. While it definitely helped and was exactly what I needed at the time, I always felt that there was something deeper I needed to express. I felt better, yet it still felt like there was something bubbling deep inside my body that I couldn't explain in words.

Once again, I was experiencing healing in layers, like peeling back the layer of an onion, and realizing that some layers are thicker than others. I managed to heal a thick enough layer through counselling for my eating disorder that I felt significant relief and my symptoms of disordered eating slowly reduced in frequency. I was determined to heal, and I would challenge any thoughts that came into my mind around food and deprivation. I also experienced a great deal of emotion rising to the surface: guilt, shame, blame, fear, grief, and worry. I was doing "all the right things," such as journaling, writing poetry, and exercising every day. As a fitness instructor, I was passionate about teaching others how to eat healthy and exercise regularly. I started teaching a large number of fitness classes and still did my own workouts. One day, I realized my relationship to food was improving, but my focus on exercising was becoming more compulsive. I would exercise every day for a couple of hours. If I was standing, waiting for the stove to heat up, I would do squats. I thought I was maintaining good nutrition by watching calories, until I realized my ego was counting calories. I felt the deep fear of gaining weight, still held in my body in the area of my lower belly.

My ego was disguising itself as my nutrition and exercise coach. Another layer of unwinding was necessary and I slowly changed my relationship to exercise. I had to let go of everything I thought I knew and begin to listen to my body. As an anorexic, I had learned to disconnect from my body. I ignored my body completely, because I hated everything about it. At this point in my healing, I realized that I needed to learn to trust my body and begin to heal it. I realized I couldn't just heal my mind, I had to unwind the long-held patterns in my body as well.

As humans, we are taught to bury our pain deep inside. The old "out of sight, out of mind" logic serves us for a period of time. The challenge is that most of us are carrying issues from early childhood that are heavy and painful, and we can only bury so much until it starts to overflow or we explode like a volcano to create space and temporary relief. Once we create space, we start to bury more and more. We learn how to deny or hide our emotions, and are taught to fear what others might think. These are all ego's ploys to keep us in a state of fear, pain, and suffering.

Emotions are designed to be expressed and released. Emotion means energy in motion. When you deny the expression of emotions, or even words, they are stored in the physical body. Uncried tears often remain in the throat. The energy centre in the throat is associated with our ability to speak our truth and express ourselves fully; that includes emotional expression. Unexpressed grief and sadness fill the lungs. Long-held anger and resentment are stored in the hips and liver. Panic and fear cause a holding pattern in the psoas muscle that leads to hip pain and pelvic instability. Guilt and shame are held deep in the pelvis, as well as the middle and lower back. Unexpressed emotions are ticking time bombs in the body, held in deep patterns of tension, tightness, and pain that ultimately lead to dis-ease.

Psychiatrist Dr. Peter Levine talks about the flight, fight, or freeze response in his book, *Waking the Tiger* (published by North Atlantic Books in 1997). Animals in the wild that experience trauma will instinctively shake the energy out of the body. If you have ever witnessed two cats fighting, you will know that once they finish, each one will walk away and give its entire body a shake. An animal that is about to be attacked in the wild will freeze and if it escapes it will find a safe spot to shake the trauma out of its body. Nature provides evidence that holding onto the energy of trauma is not the norm. Humans hold onto it. Why? Because we are taught to bury, deny, and hold onto these emotional energies in our body. This feeds the ego, because the last thing the ego wants you to do is feel your emotions fully. The ego knows that when the body is in chaos, the mind is in chaos as well. There is no clarity in confusion and chaos. Alignment with Spirit is much more challenging, and internal guidance is difficult to hear, when there is so much of a racket going on in the mind and body. This is where the process of unwinding can act as a powerful tool for healing. When you remain curious through this process, you allow space for whatever needs to release and heal.

> "When you hold on to your history, you do it at the expense of your destiny." Bishop Thomas Dexter Jakes, bishop and chief pastor of the non-denominational American megachurch "The Potter's House."

When I was away from home for ten days taking a yoga therapy training course, it was the longest time I had ever left my newborn son, my stepdaughter, and my husband. Inevitably, during that time, my mind was busy and I was easily distracted by my thoughts wandering in all directions. In the course, participants worked on each other's bodies, and as we did so we released many deeply held patterns. My physical symptoms were improving every day.

On day eight, we were guided into a centring exercise and asked to set an intention for the day. My mind was blank. Yes, it was absolutely blank for the first time in as long as I could remember. Nothing, nada, not a word in sight, and I was in awe. When asked to share my intention, I didn't want any words to come in, because I was feeling such peace and relief with the space in my mind. So my intention that day was "space." I healed and cleared so much old trauma from my body through yoga therapy, that I finally found clarity and peace of mind. Most of my childhood trauma was held in my physical body, so unwinding my physical body became the key to healing at the deepest possible level. No words were necessary, only the expression of physical symptoms and layers of emotion. When I began my practice as a yoga therapist, I discovered that profound and miraculous healing occurs to everyone when I bring them out of their heads and into their physical bodies.

Today, as an intuitive healer, I often go through the body and bypass the mind to allow for deep healing. Unwinding is not a logical process. It will not make sense in the mind. That is why I find that talk therapy sometimes becomes limiting. Why wasn't talk therapy enough for me and so many of my clients? It was helpful to talk it all out; but there was another layer that needed to be addressed. Almost every client who came to see me had healed past trauma mentally and emotionally, yet still felt stuck or blocked on some level they couldn't explain. This is where I discovered that if the body gets left behind, you will not heal at the deepest possible level. My work deepened when I began to integrate energy healing into my yoga therapy sessions and yoga classes.

There was still part of me that wanted to understand how, why, and what was happening during unwinding. When I was finally able to unwind from "needing to know" completely, I moved into a space of deep trust and curiosity. I surrendered my hands, body, mind, and soul, and allowed Spirit to lead me completely. Words, energy, movement, yoga—everything I needed to help facilitate the deepest healing for my clients—showed up with divine timing. This is when miracles began happening and I was humbled by the love that flowed through me. I was honoured to be witness to such incredible transformations and healing. My mind was wide open, and I became a clear and perfect channel for divine healing energy and love.

A Life Without Regret

Can you imagine a life free from regret? Do you believe it is possible? If you already live a life without regret, do you understand why you can embrace this perspective? When we follow our heart and when Spirit is our guide, we will live a life without regret. When we are filled with regret, we are choosing to align with ego. Remember, ego works in the past and fills our mind and heart with "would have, could have, and should have". You can use the "For Giving" section in Chapter Four to help you release any past regrets and align with Spirit from this moment forward. If you do, I promise you will never feel regret again.

The only regret from my past that I have in my awareness is one that is purposeful for teaching this concept. In April 2001, I had visited my Dad; I had a sense that he was having some health issues. A few months later, as Father's Day approached, the thought of sending my Dad a card came into my awareness. Immediately, my ego came in to remind me of why I had stopped making him Father's Day cards a long time ago, and how much pain was associated with that. When I was a little girl, my entire class would make something special each Father's Day. For a few years, I would participate with hope of seeing my Dad on Father's Day and giving him my gift. It was a fool's hope because, up until Grade Five, I only saw my Dad once a year and it was rarely on any special occasions. Each year I would make something and each year it would sit in my room until I eventually threw it out. One year, I started making all my Father's Day gifts for my Mom, because in my eyes she was playing both roles. I felt relief and buried my disappointment.

In 2001, when I received guidance to mail my Dad a card, I

quickly dismissed it because my ego was reminding me of past pain. I had already done a lot healing around my relationship with my father, but it took some time to forgive and let go of the past memories around Father's Day. In spite of healing my past, for some reason I never did send him a card. Later that summer my father passed away, and regret filled my heart. If only I had followed my intuition, he would have known I was thinking about him. If only I had sent the card, he would have realized how much I loved him.

I tell this story from a perspective of regret, but I have forgiven myself for not following my intuition. Shortly after my Dad passed away, I had a dream where he was sitting at a table smiling at me. He looked so healthy and happy. For days after, I felt my father's spirit, and I was able to communicate my regret and let him know how much I love him.

If from this moment forward you follow your heart and trust your intuition, you will live a life without regret. To heal past regret, you can use the following exercise.

♥ Heart Work: Releasing Regret

Healing our past begins by becoming present in this moment. We can't heal the past in the past. We can only heal how we feel about the past in the present moment.

Invite eight deep centring breaths. Invite a curious mindset to dissolve all judgment. Take a moment to reflect on any area of your life, relationship, or past behaviour that you feel regret toward. Begin writing about your regret in your journal. Allow everything that is inside of you to be expressed, similar to the process of emptying. Once you feel empty of thoughts, emotions, and any other forms of regret, take a moment to reflect on the lesson you gained from that experience. Imagine taking the gem or lesson into your heart and surrounding it with gratitude. Now visualize yourself releasing the anchor, freeing yourself from regret and any other thoughts and beliefs about that past experience.

Why Am I Here?

Have you ever asked the question, "Why am I here?" or "What is the purpose of my life?" I have asked those questions over and over again throughout my life. We are programmed to seek and search for answers, as we all yearn for meaning in our lives. Those who discover it thrive, those who don't, die with their music still in them.

After my father passed away, I was sorting through some old boxes filled with his belongings. I discovered old photos he had taken. My sister reminded me that one of the bedrooms in the apartment we had lived in was converted into my father's dark room for developing all his photos. I came across one of his most popular photos, taken of me and my sister under the Christmas tree when I was just under two years old. It was a black and white, and it captured the moment so brilliantly, I actually used it as the cover of a Christmas card that same year.

The sadness came when I realized my father had never lived his life on purpose. He had talents and gifts that he never really shared with the world. All that was left of his passion for photography was a box full of old photos and negatives. He died with his music still in him. I began to wonder what else there was deep in his heart that he could have shared. I thought about how different his life would have been if only he had discovered his sense of purpose and followed his passion.

So many people leave this earth without writing the book they were meant to write, or creating the business idea or product they thought they might create. It is not only sad for them, but unfortunate for all of us who remain, because the rest of the world will miss out on their undelivered gift.

What gift are you meant to share? What talents are you meant to perform to inspire and empower others? What messages are you destined to speak? We are all here for a reason, every one of us. You are not a mistake. You are not a burden. You are here because there is a purpose for your life.

> You are not a mistake. You are not a burden. You are here because there is a purpose for your life.

As I have already mentioned, since December 2012, I have noticed a significant increase in planetary energy. Energy is rising and moving faster than ever before and everyone is being called on to align with their purpose. Those who are in alignment with their purpose are experiencing the miracles that come from living with purpose. Those who are in denial, are oblivious, or are ignoring their calling are struggling big time. We are at a point in our evolution when you can either answer the calling and share your gift with the world, or you sit in the pain and suffering of resistance. I am witnessing a great deal of pain for those who are in resistance. I have empathy for them and, at the same time, I know if they would only say YES to their purpose, their entire experience of life would be transformed. I have seen people who have had overnight success the moment they align with their life's purpose.

When I discovered my life's purpose was to inspire and empower healing in myself and others, my world opened up. I felt a sense of direction, as I was no longer wandering around in the dark. I was living on purpose and no longer by default. I knew deep in my heart, body, and soul that I was here to help others heal. It doesn't matter if I am writing, speaking, teaching, coaching, or sitting beside someone, my intention is focused on healing. For years, I taught Pre- and Post-Natal Fitness Certification courses for personal trainers and group fitness instructors. I always had tissues on hand, because I knew there would be tears for the purpose of healing. You can't learn from me without healing some aspect of yourself. My intention and purpose is crystal clear. The vehicle through which I express my purpose has changed and evolved over the years, and instead of working one-on-one, I am doing more group healings in which I speak to audiences all around the world.

When you discover your purpose, it becomes the centre around which everything you do revolves. Your purpose is like the Sun. If you tune in and trust your intuition, it will lead you to the vehicles for sharing your purpose with the world. This book is part of my purpose, my speaking career, intuitive healing, yoga, motherhood, etc. Every aspect of your life will revolve around your purpose. No wonder everyone is seeking clarity around it. It is the basis that influences every decision you will make. If you are clear about your purpose, then continue to follow your heart to find your particular vehicle for sharing your purpose. If you are not clear about why you are here on this earth plane, the following exercise will help you.

♥ Heart Work: Finding Your Purpose

Answer the following questions. Remember, be curious without judgment. Write the first answers that pop into your mind. Let the answer flow, without taking time to think. This allows you to tap into your intuitive heart. The heart knows more than you think. When you tap into the intuitive heart, you are tapping into the universal source energy I call Spirit. Some of the answers may surprise you, while others you will realize you knew all along.

1. What excites you?
2. What brings you joy?
3. What feeds your soul?
4. If money wasn't an issue, what would you be doing?
5. If you had more money to spend, how would you be of service to the world?
6. What are you most passionate about?
7. What are you most grateful for?
8. What makes your heart dance?

After you allow the answers to flow through your fingers onto paper, take eight deep breaths with the intention of aligning with your purpose. Review your answers and circle words or themes that are repeated. Highlight what phrase or answer stands out the most. Is there anything that makes your cells jump or your heart expand? Feel into the answer, and be curious and wide open to any insights that come. Be willing to marinate in your answers until you are guided to revisit them or till more clarity comes. Often clarity comes within a few days of this exercise. Sometimes it will show up in a conversation with someone, an article or book you read, or something that you see in a movie or in everyday life.

Be open, be curious, and be willing. Let your heart lead you and trust your intuition. When you follow your heart, it will lead to your passion; when you follow your passion, it will lead to your purpose. The truth is our purpose is all the same at the deepest level. Our purpose is alignment with Spirit and letting our heart take the lead. If everyone in the world was in alignment all the time and that was their only purpose the world would be a very different place. I share more about this in Chapter Nine.

> When you follow your heart, it will lead to your passion; when you follow your passion, it will lead to your purpose.

I Am Enough!

Your life is a reflection of your deep-seated beliefs. In other words, your external environment is a reflection of your internal environment. If you believe life is about peace, joy, and abundance, that will be your experience and your reality. If you believe that you are not worthy of love and abundance, then your life will reflect that. My mentor Les Brown always says, "When your desires and your beliefs are not in alignment, you will always manifest what you believe."

Growing up, I had a deep-seated belief that I wasn't good enough. I wasn't smart enough, skinny enough, pretty enough, strong enough, patient enough, etc., etc., etc. The list went on and on. The only thing I can say that didn't apply to this was my height. I never felt I wasn't tall enough. I liked being short. My "not good enough" mindset began at a very young age and was deeply rooted in unworthiness. While it served me in some areas of my life, it was devastating in others. It motivated me to do more, be more, and achieve more. I became a highly effective workaholic. I worked hard and appeared very successful from the outside, but always settled living with very little money.

My belief drove me to constantly prove my worth to the world, feeding my desire to help others. It served me when I wanted to achieve something. I would set my mind to it, push through all resistance, and get it done. When I said I was going to do something, I did it. I never stopped to acknowledge or celebrate my successes, because I would look at my achievements through the lens of "not good enough." I would look for how I could have done it better or how I could improve next time. As a perfectionist, I wanted everything to be perfect, but through the "not good enough" lens nothing was ever perfect because it wasn't good enough. This is a recipe for disaster. On an energetic level it kept me from feeling complete with anything, because there was always room for improvement. Even when I went on to the next task, I still held on to the niggling that it was done but still wasn't good enough. It was as if I left everything complete but unfinished. Even though I did the best I could with the time and resources I had, my ego always came in with the thought that I could have done better. The bottom line was nothing would ever be good enough, because I wasn't enough.

Take a moment to reflect on your last project or accomplishment. Did you take a moment to acknowledge and celebrate your success? Do you ever pat yourself on the back and say, "Good job" or "I did my best" or "Well done"? Society would say that bragging is not polite or proper etiquette. That is the ego mindset.

Spirit would say, "Celebrate your successes; celebrate your life; celebrate YOU; celebrate everything, because you are a miracle!" When is the last time you tooted your own horn? How it is received is often determined by which teacher you are aligned with at the time. If you are aligned with ego, it won't be well received. Others will feel you are boasting or bragging in a way that makes others feel badly about themselves, or they get the message that you think you are better than them. If you are aligned with Spirit, people will feel your genuine authentic desire to share. Not everyone will celebrate with you, but that is none of your business. Not everyone is capable of celebrating your successes because they don't know how to do it for themselves, let alone for others. The key is to share when your heart guides you to. The most important celebration needs to happen in your own heart and mind.

Now let's look more deeply at the beliefs you hold about yourself. Keep in mind, these are not innate beliefs; these are beliefs you acquired throughout your life. It is likely that most of them were established in early childhood, although some of them are familial, passed on from generation to generation. The good news is that you can heal these past beliefs and generational patterns by healing their roots in your spiritual body. Here is an exercise to help you create awareness and release beliefs that are no longer serving you.

❤ Heart Work: Exploring Self

1. What do you believe about yourself?
2. When others compliment you, do you receive it with your whole heart and say thank you?
3. What do you believe is possible for your life?
4. Do you believe in unlimited potential or in limitations?
5. Are you worthy of love, happiness, joy, and abundance?
6. Do you realize that you are greater than your physical body?
7. Do you know that you have something unique and special to share with the world?
8. Do you recognize that your life matters?

As you explore your answers to these questions, be open and curious about any niggling deep inside. Remember, resistance is the gap between what your mind thinks and what your heart knows. Your heart knows you are worthy. Your heart knows that YOU are ENOUGH. Your heart knows you are perfect. If your mind is not in alignment with that truth, you will feel it either emotionally, physically, or energetically. When you remain curious, you will be able to tune into the resistance sooner rather than later. If you have trouble believing your heart, borrow my belief in you until yours kicks in.

> Your heart knows you are perfect. If your mind is not in alignment with that truth, you will feel it either emotionally, physically, or energetically.

No matter what anyone else has ever said to you or anything your ego says to you, here is the truth:

"You are enough! You are beautiful inside and out! You are extraordinary! You are unique! You are loved beyond what your mind can conceive! You are perfect just the way you are! The world is lucky to have you! You are held in a blanket of love and light! Your life matters! You deserve to live a life that you love! You deserve to wake up every morning and say, 'YES!' You are a magnificent spiritual being with a beautiful physical presence! There is so much love for you!"

Will you receive that?

Chapter 8

Heart Led Living Principle ~ Be Attached to Nothing

This is probably one of the most challenging principles to fully embrace and integrate. It requires a lot of unwinding from our conditioned thoughts and beliefs. I have been guided to use death as the tool to teach this principle. Initially, I was resistant to write this chapter because death is such a sensitive topic. After speaking to a few people, including my publisher Julie Salisbury, I realized that this is the most powerful place to begin. Whether the attachment is to a material object, a job, a relationship, a family member, a loved one, a belief, a thought, your home, animals or even your own identity, attachment equals alignment with the ego. When we are attached to anything, we provide the ego with a point of weakness. We latch onto something or someone for fear of losing it. That fear is often paralyzing or it causes us to react and behave in self-destructive ways. When we align with Spirit and practise non-attachment, we are aligning with the truth that we are whole and complete just as we are. There is no desperate need to have someone or something in our lives to feel complete. We are going to go deep in this chapter and I ask that you stay open. Roll with any resistance and be willing to express any emotions that arise.

> Attachment equals alignment with the ego.

To Live or to Leave

Since December 2012, the Universal energy has been rising at a rapid rate and our human race is being called into a new level of consciousness. If you are answering the calling and raising your own vibration to match or move into alignment with the vibration of our planet, you will be thriving and experiencing miracles. If you resist, you will continue to align with ego and it will be painful. I am witnessing many people in resistance and their pain is deep and overwhelming, so much so that some are choosing to leave this earth plane through suicide. Others are in such deep denial that their body is shutting down. I have had several friends who have lost loved ones through sudden heart attacks, brain aneurisms, or unexplained deaths. I have spent the last couple of months exploring my relationship with death and supporting others through their grief. That exploration has allowed me to deepen in the trust and faith that everything is purposeful and for our highest good. It doesn't mean we don't feel loss or pain in our hearts, because there is still a grieving process for the loss of the physical relationship with that person. It means that we can be open to find meaning as we negotiate our way through loss.

I have been focused on healing my past wounds and aligning with my heart's path since 1993. It has been a slow and steady process up until this last year when I felt a quickening and sense of urgency to heal as deeply as I could as fast as possible. I believe it was because I am meant to help usher others over the bridge, so that it isn't so painful if they choose to leave. Whatever choice you make, there is a great amount of love waiting for you.

I have been shown that there are two reasons people choose to leave the earth plane. The first is that their work is done here and their soul is ready to return to the spiritual realm. Or they are so lost and disconnected from their truth that they believe they can't possibly find their way back into the light. The latter is not true, but to the person experiencing it, that appears to be their only option. The ego has burrowed deeply in their mind like a virus and is extremely convincing. I have helped people out of really dark places and supported them as they found their alignment again. I have witnessed many miracles and transformations in a very short time. What is possible for one is possible for all.

I have great compassion and empathy for everyone and at the same time I choose to see their potential. I choose to hold them in the light. I choose to inspire and empower them to say "YES" to life. Spirit shows me their light and the love that is available to them. I can only hope they find it here on this earth plane, but it is not up to me to decide for others. That is where the non-attachment comes in as a practice in self-care and soul care. I can hold a vision and show others what is possible for them. I can share my story and give them hope that if I can overcome everything that I have overcome, they can too. I can surround them with a blanket of love and let them know they don't need to do it alone. In the end, it is up to them to walk to the edge of life and make their own choices. Whatever they choose, I will love them either way.

For the Love of Death

The idea of death seems to be a great mystery that we have been taught to fear. As a society, we are conditioned to fear the un-known. What happens when we die? Where do we go? Why is it so painful to lose someone? If death is a natural part of the cycle of life and is embraced in nature, why do we fear it so much as humans?

I grew up terrified and paranoid when it came to the subject of death, but in the last ten years, and more so in the last two years, my relationship with death has changed completely. Today, I am very curious and open to a new perspective. What if you could allow Spirit to lead you through the experience of death? Are you open to a new perspective? This is a challenging chapter for me to write because I know there is so much fear and pain around death. As you read the stories, I invite you to remain open and curious without judgment or attachment to what you know about death. Be willing to see it afresh from a new lens, even if it is just for this brief chapter.

In the fall of 2012, my eighty-nine-year-old paternal grandfather refused to eat and was taken to the hospital for IV fluids. He was confused, anxious, and afraid. He kept pulling out his IV and the nurses told my Grandma that if he didn't cooperate, they would be forced to send him back to the retirement home. At first I was angry. Do you send a two-year-old home when they need hospital care, because they aren't cooperating? Where is the empathy here? Then I heard a voice deep in my heart, "He doesn't want to be helped. It is his time to leave." NO! Not my Grandfather! Tears flowed down my cheeks, but I knew it was true. It was his time. It was his choice and I needed to honour that.

It took all my strength, faith, and trust to stay home and not book a flight to be with my grandparents. Every day, I would look at flights but my heart kept telling me to wait. He was sent home from the hospital and, as the weeks passed, my grandfather continued to refuse food. His body became weaker and weaker. Every day while in meditation, I would tune into his spirit and I would receive messages from him. One morning I heard his voice as clear as if he were in the room with me. I was tempted to open my eyes and see, but I didn't want to interfere with the connection I had. He said to me, "My belle fille, my body is weak and my mind is tired. It is time for me to go. Wait to come. Grandma will need you after I leave."

Further insight came. I knew if I went to be by his side it would be harder for him to leave. It was already hard enough for him to leave his lifelong love. In the meantime, I prayed for his transition to be kind and painless. I spoke to my Grandma every day by phone to get an update and give her my support. I can only imagine how difficult it was each day, as she watched the love of her life weakening and letting go.

My grandparents had been married for sixty-seven years, and they were just as much in love as the day they had first met. They would hold hands and kiss all the time. My Grandpa would always tease and joke, and they laughed together a lot. Everyone commented about how much they loved each other and how precious it was to see them together with such a spark after all those years. Their love is what inspires me in my own marriage.

On Friday, September 14, I spoke to my Grandma and she felt my Grandpa's death was close. I had a sense he would pass after the weekend. My heart was still telling me to wait to book my flight, although I felt strongly I would be flying on Monday. I waited for a clear heart YES with infinite patience. On Sunday, my Grandma told me she was ready to let him go. In my meditation that night I told my Grandpa goodbye for now and that it was okay to leave. As much as my heart was breaking at the loss of our physical connection, I knew that he would still communicate with me in spirit, the same way my Dad continues to come through in my dreams, and comes as a hummingbird at my window. At 6:00 a.m. on Monday morning, the phone rang. It was my sister telling me Grandpa had passed away that morning. I found the first flight available to be there for my Grandma.

I arrived early Tuesday morning and spent the day with my grandmother. She seemed strong and determined to get everything that needed to be done finished for the funeral. Around 5:00 p.m., we sorted through my Grandpa's belongings and we packed what my Grandma wanted to keep into a few boxes. We spent some time looking through old photos, and sharing stories and memories of the summers we had spent at their cottage each year. Around 9:00 p.m., my sister, brother, and their kids arrived. We all visited with Grandma until about 10:00 p.m. She looked tired, so we left her to get a good night's sleep. We were all staying just up the road from the retirement home with my Grandpa's sister Rose.

And Then, the Unthinkable Happened...

Around midnight, I heard my Aunt Rose's phone ringing. At first, I thought I shouldn't answer the phone when she wasn't there. But suddenly I felt this huge jolt, almost like I was being pushed out of bed and directed to the phone. When I answered, I heard my Aunt Lise say, "Grandma is in the hospital. They think she is having a heart attack!" Noooooooooo! This can't be happening! As I rushed to the hospital, the only words that rang through my mind were, "No, no, no, no, no! Why? Please tell me this isn't happening."

My grandmother and I are very close. She means the world to me. Growing up, she was such a beacon of light, hope, and wisdom in my life. My Grandma loves with her whole heart. She had a way of making me feel like I was the most special person in her life. At bedtime she would come and tuck me in. She would kiss me, and say, "Goodnight, my Queen of Sheba." I felt so loved and special. I realized when I got older that she made everyone feel that way. She showed me what unconditional love looks and feels like. In her eyes, I was her "Queen of Sheba", and she made me feel like I was always a good little girl. Even when I did something wrong, I felt her love for me was unwavering.

When I arrived at the hospital, I knew it was not looking good. I called my brother and sister to come right away. Grandma was on oxygen and I could tell she was in a lot of pain. With tears in our eyes and love in our hearts, my siblings and I were allowed to go to her bedside for a brief moment. She grabbed all our hands and brought them to her heart. We all told her how much we love her, and her eyes filled with tears. I believe if we hadn't all been present at that time, she wouldn't have made it through the night.

We all stayed in the hospital that night. We still needed to continue planning my grandfather's funeral, so just one of us stayed with Grandma throughout the day at all times. After speaking to a number of close relatives, we all decided it would be best to continue with the funeral plans even though my grandmother wouldn't be attending. For the rest of the day, Grandma would come in and out of consciousness. In her weakened state, she kept saying that Grandpa was calling her. She said to my sister, "Two at a time. Two at a time," meaning she was meant to leave with my grandfather.

Grandma had no history of heart disease, so everyone was shocked. She had lost the love of her life and her heart was breaking with grief. My brother, sister, and I all knew we had to give her permission to leave. At eighty-eight years of age, she wanted to be with her love and I understood that. I whispered into her ear, "I love you, Grandma, with all my heart. If you want to be with Grandpa, I understand. I will miss you deeply, but it's okay for you to go. I will love you no matter what you choose."

For two days, she was in intensive care, and at one point, she asked for the priest to come and pray for her. Many of us stood around her bed, holding hands, joining our hearts to pray for her life. I was praying to give her the courage to make the choice that was best for her. A few hours later, I was at my grandfather's funeral with tears streaming down my face. I wasn't sure who I was crying for. Part of me was grieving the loss of an amazing and respected hero in my life, my grandfather. The other part of me was grieving for the possibility of having to say goodbye to my grandmother.

After the funeral, I returned to the hospital. As I sat by my Grandma's bedside, I knew that if she was going to leave it would be that night. I was hopeful, but at the same time, I prepared myself for her to choose to be with my Grandpa. I was guided to sleep at my Aunt's that night. I slept with the phone by my side. The next morning, I arrived at the hospital and she had been moved out of ICU. She was actually sitting up in bed when I entered her room. The first thing she said was, "The food here is terrible. It's always cold. I want to go home." I laughed with pure joy, because I knew in my heart she had chosen to stay.

That week was one of the most emotionally intense times in my life. I was so grateful to be heart-led through it all and to have the phone support of my heart-led friend Lisa. Only four or five years ago, that experience would have been so much more painful, because I would have been in a suffering state of mind, walking through it with my ego. This time, I walked with faith and trusted that everything was happening for a reason. I followed my heart, was unattached to the outcome, and stayed present to each moment. I processed the emotions as they surfaced and gave myself permission to feel fully without judgment.

> Only four or five years ago, that experience would have been so much more painful, because I would have been in a suffering state of mind, walking through it with my ego. This time, I walked with faith and trusted that everything was happening for a reason.

The biggest lesson came shortly after I returned home. I realized that it is not up to me to convince anyone to choose life. Wanting someone else to live is not enough. They need to choose life. It is a choice they need to make in their heart.

I Give You Full Permission to Leave

Imagine if we were all able to hold space for someone to choose to live or to leave. What if your only intention was to help them hear the truth in their heart? Would you be able to love them, even if they chose to leave?

Since that experience with my grandparents, I have had a number of clients come to me struggling with thoughts of suicide. I was curious about why, all of a sudden, death was showing up once more. Several times I was guided to walk them to the edge of life, giving them full permission to choose: to live or to leave. If you leave, there is great love for you, and if you stay, there is great love for you. As they stood on the edge, they felt a sense of relief followed by empowerment and peace. No one had ever allowed them to walk to the edge and make a choice. They hadn't even done that for themselves. Their ego kept them wondering, pondering, and contemplating with fear, worry, and anxiety, but they were never courageous enough to walk to the edge. I was guided to be a spiritual witness and hold a sacred space of non-judgment and unconditional love, as they looked over the edge and gave themselves full permission to choose.

Thankfully, all of my clients have chosen life. After each session, they felt a renewed sense of purpose and an awakened desire to live. At first, I had moments of worry. What if they choose to leave? Am I giving them permission to commit suicide? When I return to trust and allow the divine Spirit within to lead me through each session, I know this is part of my life's work. I trust this process because I feel I am being guided through it. There is a voice and energy coming through me. It is not me, but Spirit speaking to them through me. I am simply a messenger of the light, hope, and possibility for their life.

Cry All Uncried Tears

Earlier this year, our female Olde Boston Bulldogge had three puppies: two with life and one without. The two with life appeared healthy: they started breastfeeding right away. We named the little girl Roxy and the boy Cooper. On day four after their birth, I found the young male lying on his side gasping for air. I immediately picked him up and ran upstairs to find my husband. The puppy was turning blue, so I knew he wasn't getting enough oxygen. I gave him a few breaths using a mouth to nose technique I learned as a Veterinary Technician. His colour improved slightly, but he was still struggling. I told my husband he needed oxygen. I held the puppy in my arms, wrapped in a warm towel, and we drove to meet some friends who had an oxygen tank we could borrow. Once in my arms, his breathing became a little easier. The oxygen tank was huge compared to the tiny weakened puppy in my hands. I held the tubing to his nose and his colour improved a bit more.

I reached out to Lisa for support, as thoughts of worry and fear were sneaking in. She reminded me of how I walked to the edge of life with my father, grandparents, and clients. This was no different. I knew in my heart I needed to hold the puppy in love, and give him permission to choose. No heroics. Simply send him love and give him permission to live or leave. The moment

I sent that message from my heart to his, I watched him take his last peaceful breath. Part of me hoped he would take another, but I knew he had chosen to leave. I was grateful for the oxygen because his last breath was peaceful and easy. It was as though he fell asleep and his spirit peacefully left his body.

Although his life was brief, he left an imprint in my heart. I cried a little that night. My nine year old son came up to me and said, "It's okay, Mom. Sometimes, these things happen."

My heart melted and I smiled. What a wise soul. The next morning I found myself bawling on the floor in a fetal position. I thought the tears would never stop as I questioned, "How can someone cry so much about a four-day-old puppy?" I realized they were deep tears that had been brought to the surface to heal. I cried for every client, every woman who lost a child, every person I loved who had passed, everyone who is still living in grief, I cried out all the loss and sadness from deep inside my body, mind, and spirit. When the tears stopped, I sat up and felt a deep sense of relief and a beautiful awakening. It was as if I was looking at everything through a new set of eyes. All I could see was the beauty, love, and light that surrounded me. I released anything and everything that was not in alignment with Spirit, and once again I gave myself permission to say "YES" to life! What a gift!

Just when we believe we have learned the lesson, Spirit comes in and encourages us to deepen our faith and trust. Certain lessons will continue to show up as gentle reminders about what we already know, and plant the new seeds of what we still need to learn. We are either learning new lessons or deepening the current ones. As I write this book, my lessons around death continue and my perspective continues to evolve. The learning around death began when I was guided to walk to the edge of my own life and question, "Why am I here and what is the purpose of my life?" Now I can support others in facing their fears around death, helping them unwind from the hold ego has on their mind and assisting them in tuning into the truth in their heart. I can't decide what is on someone else's path, but I can certainly encourage them to follow their heart and trust in their intuition, regardless of what others think.

♥ Heart Work: Walking to the Edge of Life

Journal about walking to the edge of your life. Write down all your fears, judgments, anxiety, concerns, grief, and any other emotions that surround the subject of death. Explore areas of life you feel attached to. Are you attached to certain people, animals or even things like your home, etc. Being attached means on a deep level you are afraid to lose it. Allow your fears about death to surface and give yourself permission to feel any emotions that arise. Emotions must be expressed, not held back. Let all the feelings wash up and out. Our ego does not want us to walk to the edge of life and discover that we actually have a choice to live or to leave. Our ego depends on us buying into our fear about death. When we look death straight on, it is not as scary as our ego would have us believe. Some people need to walk to the edge and see that there is a life worth living. When we live in fear of death, the fear keeps us paralyzed. When we face our own death, we free ourselves to say, "YES!" to life.

Continue to journal and express any and all emotions that surface. Be willing to feel in order to heal. If you need support through this process, you can contact me for a private session through my website at www.heartledliving.com. Remember that there is great love for you. You are stronger than you realize and more courageous than you think.

> Be willing to feel in order to heal.

Chapter 9

Heart Led Living Principle ~ Lead With Your Heart

We hear people say it all the time: just follow your heart. Sounds simple, but it is not always easy. Some people seem to do it naturally or purposefully, some by default and for others it is a completely foreign concept. When we consciously choose to follow our heart, we tap into an unlimited source of divine wisdom. It is our direct connection to the source of all things. While our minds are limited to what our human perspective can comprehend, our hearts give us a direct link to a universal perspective that goes beyond our thinking mind. When we follow our heart, we allow the Spirit within us to guide us to everything our heart desires and so much more than we could ever begin to imagine.

Get Out of Your Head and Into Your HEART

We are taught by society to think, analyze, and be reasonable. We are conditioned to live in our heads and make logical decisions based on facts and reason. We weren't born logical. We were all born being in touch with our intuitive heart. Originally, we couldn't communicate our needs, desires, or fears. We learned them.

We have one intuitive heart and two minds. Our two minds are our conscious and subconscious minds. Our conscious mind is responsible for activities like decision making, analyzing, and creating future plans or our to-do list. This is the area of our minds where we can become aware of our self-talk or chatter. According to psychologists, we think only 5% of the 60,000 thoughts we have each day in our conscious mind. The remaining

95% of our thoughts arise from our subconscious mind. I see the subconscious mind being like a continuous tape repeatedly playing all our limiting thoughts and beliefs. All our deep-rooted beliefs about what is possible for our lives reside here. It is also referred to as the emotional mind. Every desire we have in our conscious mind is filtered through the subconscious mind. If our desires are not in alignment with our beliefs, then we experience resistance.

According to Dr. Bruce Lipton, author of *The Biology of Belief* (published by Hay House in 2008), we don't have access to our ability to reason until the development of our conscious mind around the age of six-years old. Up until that time, we are essentially downloading everything without questioning its truth or validity. We are born perfect and then programmed based on our environment, which is often based on fear, lack, and limitation. For example, when I grew up, I learned that there was never enough money and that you had to work hard to earn more. As children we were taught to "be careful" and "watch you don't fall". The messages we received, although well intended, were mostly based on fear. The ego weasels its way into our subconscious mind as early as conception and it feeds on the fear in our environment to instill even more fear deep in our minds.

I attended a workshop on transitions and movement based on the developmental phases of a baby, who goes from rolling over, to sitting, to crawling, and eventually to standing. During that workshop we did a movement exploration exercise in which one person would be a baby in the womb, and the rest of the group would act as the uterus, providing resistance with their arms and hands. When it was my turn I was fascinated by the fluid movement I could experience with the support of the group around me. I closed my eyes and had vivid memories of being in my mother's uterus. Suddenly this intense fear filled my entire body and the words, "It's too quiet," blurted out of my mouth. Everyone around me was so quiet that the deep silence brought back a memory of fear.

I was curious about my uncontrolled response, so I took some time to reflect afterward. When my mother was pregnant with me, she and my father were still together. At that point in their relationship my parents argued a lot. As a baby I was in some way comforted by the yelling and the noise. At least when I heard them fighting, I knew my mother was okay. I have a memory of feeling the need to protect my mother. I could sense her fear and stress. My father was never physically abusive, but for whatever reason I became afraid of silence while in my mother's uterus. Later, I started to notice more of a pattern playing out in my life around a fear of silence. It became clear why I always needed the radio or TV playing in the background and why it was so challenging to quieten my mind: noise comforted me. With awareness I was able to heal that fear and now I welcome quiet; in fact, I rarely have music playing even when I am driving in my car.

The beliefs I developed in my childhood around money were "there is never enough" and "you can always do more". This led to my workaholic tendencies and I fell into the cycle of living paycheque to paycheque. Money would always show up if I was going to take a trip or go visit family, but there was never an abundance of money in the bank. I had just enough to get by and live comfortably. If I came into extra money, I would spend it instead of saving it.

My desire for abundance grew. Until I re-programmed my deep-seated beliefs of scarcity, I was stuck in a cycle of lack and limitation, sprinkled with stress and anxiety around my finances. Once I cleared that belief, I thought it would be easy to earn more money. I explored the resistance and discovered another deep-seated belief that wasn't in alignment with my desire for abundance: I am not worthy. I could go on and on, because in my case there were numerous blocks, beliefs, and layers that needed to heal before I could open my heart, mind, and life to abundance. The point I need you to remember is that if your desires are not coming easily and effortlessly, you need to explore some possible beliefs that may be interfering with your ability to manifest them.

♥ Heart Work: Subconscious Reprogramming

Practising subconscious reprogramming sounds simple, but it is not always easy. Our ego loves to play interference at any point of weakness it can find. Our subconscious mind can be a point of weakness, but it can also be a source of empowerment.

Every morning, look in the mirror, look directly into your eyes, and say "I choose love, because I am love." Or say, "I am a full expression of love and vibrant health." You can also repeat these, or similar statements, throughout the day until you begin to feel the shift. Suddenly, you will start to believe them on a deeper cellular and energetic level. Set an intention to reprogram your subconscious mind. Using "I choose" or "I am" at the beginning of the sentence makes these powerful reprogramming statements. If you still feel resistance, it is helpful to work with someone like me who can help you see the invisible thoughts keeping you from achieving your dreams.

Awakening Your Intuitive Heart

I mentioned that we are dealing with two minds and one intuitive heart. While healing the subconscious mind of limiting thoughts and beliefs is helpful and often necessary, there is a way to bypass both minds altogether. This is where the practice of following your intuitive heart comes in. When we follow our intuition, we are aligning with Spirit, as well as aligning with our heart's path. When your desire in your mind is in alignment with your heart's desire, it is with certainty that it will be on your heart's path. When the desire in your mind is not in alignment with your heart's desire you will not be able to manifest it, and even if you do manage to, it will be a hard, painful, and unfulfilling road.

> While healing the subconscious mind of limiting thoughts and beliefs is helpful and often necessary, there is a way to bypass both minds altogether.

There is also a way to bypass your mind by following your intuitive heart. I follow my heart even when it doesn't make sense in my head and especially when it doesn't make sense to others. We all have a built-in guidance system leading us to everything our heart desires. We get lost, side tracked, and derailed altogether when we try and figure it out in our minds. We may be clear in our conscious mind but we have no idea what is happening in our subconscious mind. Therefore, if you lead with your heart and allow your mind to follow, your path will flow with ease and grace. When challenges arise or self-sabotaging behaviour shows up, you can ask your intuitive heart to lead you back to the path you are meant to be on. Remember, intuition is a feeling deep inside. It is a knowing that goes beyond thinking.

The Birds, the Bees, and the Spiritual Seeds

"Dear God, please help me see the Truth about myself no matter how beautiful it is."

When I first heard this prayer shared by Dr. Christiane Northrup, my heart jumped with excitement that perhaps everything I believed about myself wasn't actually true. What if everything I thought I knew wasn't true? What if everything I was told as a child wasn't true? What if the perspective I saw from my human eyes was just a tiny corner of a much larger picture?

What if we could see the true beauty, magnificence, and unlimited potential that lies deep within each of us? We can often see it in others; but what if we saw it within ourselves?

I am reminded of the story some parents tell their children who ask, "Where do babies come from?" The parents tell their children about the birds and the bees, or how babies are carried by storks and delivered to their parents at night. Children are so innocent and naive. Always curious and questioning, wondering "why" and "how" things work. As I mentioned earlier, Dr. Bruce Lipton explains in his book *Biology of Belief* (published by Hay

House in 2008), that up to the age of six, we faithfully download everything we are told. Our conscious mind has not yet developed to the point where we can challenge or question what we are told. We simply download and believe that babies come from storks, or that babies suddenly and magically start growing in women's bellies.

Over time, we are taught that we are human beings meant to follow the rules of society, our parents, teachers, and other people in authority. We are taught to conform to the beliefs and systems put in place by those who came before us. It is drilled into our little minds that we should respect adults and listen to them, or there will be consequences. It doesn't take long before we begin to question our own intuition and start to rely on what others think we should or shouldn't do. We disconnect from that place within us that knows beyond thinking. We unplug from our "source" and give our lives over to society, hoping for the best.

The saddest part is that we are teaching the younger generation to distrust their innate internal guidance system. We are born innocent and then programmed for failure. What if it didn't have to be that way? What if we could teach the upcoming generation that they are perfect just the way they are? What if you could remember that you are innocent, loved, and as precious as the day you were born? What if you discovered this truth right here and now for yourself as well? It is never too late to remember and it is never too early to remind others that they are beautiful, divine, and worthy.

Let me relate to you my version of the birds and the bees, and how we came to this earth plane. I invite you to open your mind wide and remain curious. Feel into this idea and tune into any familiarity or resonance deep inside you. We may have come from an egg and a sperm in the physical realm, but we began as spiritual beings having an experience in the spiritual realm first.

I have heard Dr. Wayne Dyer speak live in Vancouver a few times and he spoke once about the idea of us choosing our parents before we were born. That really resonated deep down inside me for a number of reasons. I felt empowered by the idea that I had chosen my parents. Suddenly, I didn't feel like a victim of my circumstances. Knowing that I had made a choice to share the challenges that my parents faced lifted the burdens I carried. I embraced the idea that my soul designed my heart's path to include all those life challenges, obstacles, and hardships, so that I could learn the lessons I needed to learn. Due to the obstacles I faced, I evolved to the level I needed to reach in order to become the woman I am today. If I hadn't been so incredibly lost in pain and suffering, I wouldn't have found the brilliant light and love I experience today. WOW! That was a huge and holy shift for me!

That means that life is not happening to us; life is happening for us. It is designed to awaken us to the truth that everything is playing out in the way it needs to. This is good news, because it moves us out of the need to control, and into trust and surrender. Our life is unfolding perfectly and when we align with our heart's path, the Universe will align with us. Everything we need will show up with divine timing. All challenges and perceived obstacles are on our path to help us become aware of anything that needs to heal. All triggers and emotional challenges are opportunities to heal that which is no longer serving us.

Life is not happening to us; life is happening for us.

You are perfect and your life is unfolding perfectly, just for YOU! All you need to do is increase your awareness, follow your heart, and purposefully choose to heal everything that is being called to the surface for healing. As we heal ourselves, we contribute to the healing of the planet. How? Because we are all connected to the one source. Each of us is a unique extension of one source energy. It is that same energy that flows through each and every one of us, through everything on this earth plane and beyond. We are here to evolve, heal, and spread the truth that we are all born of love. Pain and suffering enter in when we buy into the lie that we are separate from our source. Those who feel they are dying on the inside feel that way because they are unplugged from the unlimited source of love and abundant energy fueling all our systems.

Whatever you wish to call this one source—Spirit, or God, or the Divine, or the Buddha—it is not a being that is out there somewhere: it is the light of our soul that lies within each of us. We share an interconnectedness that goes beyond what words can describe. It is not a concept many can fully understand in the mind, but you can experience it in your heart and soul as a feeling of deep love and compassion. We all come from the same source, the same Mother, and we all share an extension of that same energy. When we came to this Earth, our creator was in awe of the miracle that we were. You are still that miracle! Will you choose to remember that? You are love. You are God. You are Spirit. You are, because you are a unique extension of Spirit and you are a gift to this world.

> This one source is the light of our soul that lies within each of us.

The unique part of you is the Spiritual seed that was planted deep in your soul. It is a gift that you are meant to share with this world. It is designed to contribute to the healing of the planet. It is a unique talent, book, message, song, or other gift, which only you can deliver. It is up to you to water and nurture this seed so it can grow with divine timing. Your life matters because you are the one and only individual who can deliver this gift, which will contribute to the evolution and global healing of our planet. Some of us have bigger roles to play in the eyes of the world, but it is so important that you know every gift is needed and whether your gift seems big or small, it is equally valuable.

Life Is Occurring NOW

Every moment is a gift. That is why it is called the "present" moment. It is meant to be unwrapped with great anticipation. Take a moment to reflect on this. Most people spend each precious moment worrying about what may or may not happen in the future, or feeling guilty, or regretting decisions from the past. One could argue that the future doesn't really exist, because once it arrives it becomes the present moment. So all that exists and all we know for certain is what's happening now, and now, and now.

When I look back at my life, I was never really living in the present moment. I was constantly looking forward to something, or feeling guilt or shame about something I had done in the past. Instead of being fully present to "what is", I was always counting down days until my next trip, or visit from a friend, or something else in the future. I was so consumed with what was to come, that I was unaware of what was available to me in each moment. Life was occurring without my conscious awareness. It was as though I was walking in my sleep waiting for the next moment to arrive, only when it did arrive I was already focusing on the next, and the next, and the next moments. I was never fully present to the gifts that were right in front of me in each precious moment. Many of those gifts were left unopened. Imagine giving a beautifully wrapped present to someone and they put it on a table and never opened it.

So, if all that exists is in the present moment, why do we try and live outside that timeframe? If the secret recipe for life exists in this very moment, why do we allow our minds to keep us distracted from appreciating it fully? This is a powerful and effective distraction tactic of the ego. Our ego pulls us into regret or guilt about the past, or fear and worry about our future. The ego thrives here, and society adds to the confusion by feeding our fears and worries through all kinds of media. Ego works in both the past and the future. Spirit works only in the present moment. Remember, you are either in alignment with ego or with Spirit, never both. You are either fully present or you are not. Our ego only has power over us if we are not fully present. Spirit works in the here and now. Once you become present and aware of how you are feeling right in this moment, you are choosing to align with Spirit as your teacher. This is where you can hear your heart whispering the directions in each and every moment.

> Ego works in both the past and the future.
> Spirit works only in the present.

Reflect back on a time you travelled to another city or country, and how present you were to the surroundings. Everything was fresh and exciting. It was an adventure, and you likely savoured every moment. It is easier to be in the present moment when you are away from the day-to-day rituals and habits that lead you mindlessly through your day. When you are on vacation your mind is focused on the "now", instead of on all the things you still need to get done before bedtime, like folding laundry, scrubbing dishes, and other chores.

Being fully present while in stillness is a gift that many people don't allow themselves to experience. They feel like they are doing nothing when in fact they are being fully present. A lot happens when we practise deep awareness. Giving ourselves permission to be still allows our body a chance to rest and return to a state of harmony. It gives our mind and body time to integrate our experiences so we can process what we need to process, release what we don't need, and facilitate deep healing.

Imagine if you were as fully present in your everyday environment, as you are when you are on vacation. What if your schedule were manageable and flowing, so that you didn't feel a constant need to rush? Imagine if you had time to look at the bug your child excitedly found, or appreciate the flowers, the sky, and the mountains, or fully feel the love of a friend. What if you actually took the time to sit in awe of the miracles that are present all around? Imagine all the gifts you could begin to unwrap with joy, anticipation, and appreciation. Life is not meant to be worried away, it is meant to be cherished and appreciated. It is meant to be savoured with all of our senses. You must be fully present to appreciate all that life has to offer.

> You must be fully present to appreciate all
> that life has to offer.

The most powerful question to bring you fully present is: "What's happening now?" This is an open-ended question that allows you to be curious and wide open to any answer that comes into your awareness. You may notice something in the physical body, you may become aware of some emotions, or you may suddenly see a new perspective in your current environment. Asking this question while exploring nature will open up your eyes and mind to a whole new world of sounds, sights, smells, and colours.

I remember when I was a child walking on a nature trail; I was so fully present to nature. I loved finding bugs and little tiny critters. One day, I found a tiny frog the size of my thumb nail. It was sitting very still on a leaf at the side of the trail. Even though the frog blended in, because it was the same colour as the leaf, my eyes found it right away. When I showed everyone what I discovered their response was, "How did you ever find that?" My response was, "How could you not see it?"

Heart Work: What's Happening NOW?

You may want to practise this in nature or out of your normal environment. Sit or stand in stillness, and take eight deep breaths. Imagine your mind is wide open. Ask yourself, "What is happening now?" Be open and curious. Involve all your senses. Be fully present to anything and everything, without judgment. Simply observe.

Free to Be ME!

What would the world be like if we all gave each other permission to be ourselves? How would your life be different if you were free to be YOU? Most people live their lives trying to be what others expect them to be. Or they are constantly trying to fit in. The problem is you don't fit into anyone else's expectations and you never will. We are all unique expressions of one source energy and we were created for a reason. Judy Garland wrote, *"Always be a first rate version of yourself, not a second rate version of someone else"*.

For the longest time I wanted to be anyone else but me. I was always striving to live up to others' expectations of me and it got to the point that I completely lost myself. I was so busy wearing masks and pretending to be everything everyone else wanted me to be, that I no longer knew who I was. When I really started to embrace the idea that my life mattered, I was able to start finding myself once again. I went from dying on the inside, to discovering my YES for life. As I found self-love and compassion, my faith deepened and I was able to discover the YES for MY life. I am not who I used to be, yet I am more myself today, and that is the vision I hold for you.

> Self-love is the key and is where all healing begins.

Are you willing to be a full expression of self? If you felt a heart YES, then that means you are willing to be a full expression of love. You are perfect love! You were born perfect and you remain perfect. It is only in your mind that you believe you are not. In your heart and soul you know this truth. I am simply shining light on the truth deep inside you. I give you full permission to be YOU! And the rest of the world needs you to be YOU. When you align fully with your heart's path and become a full expression of YOU, everything aligns and you create a ripple effect that will be felt all around the world. Love is the highest vibrational resonance available at this time. There is a lot of love in the world and up until this point it hasn't been enough to heal the planet. Self-love is the key and is where all healing begins. The more you love yourself, the deeper you can love others. When you love yourself unconditionally you are contributing to a rise in the level of love in the world.

> "We are not held back by the love we didn't receive in the past, but by the love we're not extending in the present," (Facebook post by Marianne Williamson, spiritual teacher).

Free yourself from judgment. Release all fears and make a conscious choice in favour of LOVE. You deserve more love than you can even begin to imagine. You are perfect love and Spirit sees you in that truth. You don't need healing. Actually, in the eyes of Spirit, you are already healed. There is nothing wrong with you; in fact, everything is right. You are perfect. You are perfect just the way you are. That is how I choose to see everyone. I see the love deep inside their heart. I see beyond the pain and see a vibrant being ready to shine brightly in this world. I see your potential. I see your true nature. I see your soul ready to express itself fully on this earth plane. I see YOU, and you are more beautiful than you could ever imagine! I see you, and you are brilliant, vibrant, and perfect! I see YOU! You are free to be a full expression of YOU! You are free to be YOU; I am free to be ME; and together we will raise the level of love in this world. You just need to say, "YES!"

Follow Your Heart's Path

It is never too late to discover your heart's path. You have arrived here precisely when you were meant to. Some of us have had to learn the hard way (that was me), while others stumble upon their path with more ease and grace. Either way, you arrived here in this moment on the path that was meant for your deepest healing. You didn't do your life all wrong. In fact, you did everything all right! Everything up until this moment was designed to heal at the deepest possible level and awaken your soul so you can discover your YES for life!

> "Embryos turn into babies; buds turn into blossoms; acorns turn into oak trees. The same programming that exists in them exists in each of us -- to manifest our highest potential. What is the difference between those things and us? That we can say no ... So today, say yes." Facebook post by Marianne Williamson, spiritual teacher.

It is ego judgment that declares we did it wrong in the past or aren't doing it right in the present. It is judgment that leads us to question our soul. What we did in the past is not important. What is important is what we are choosing right now. An acorn doesn't judge the chaos that occurs when it begins to break open under the earth's soil. A tree doesn't feel embarrassed if it is growing sideways and it doesn't look the same as all the other trees. It doesn't judge itself, and neither should we. Nature, in all of its beautiful and unique expressions, is non-judgmental.

Our heart doesn't judge; only ego judges. The moment we hear a thought of judgment or feel any level of resistance, that aware-ness becomes an opportunity to heal. Remember healing occurs in the present moment. You can heal right NOW and at every moment that arrives in the present. It is a choice you make in your mind and a commitment you align with in your heart. Be open and curious as you let your emotional compass give you cues about your alignment. Challenge all thoughts that are not in alignment with Spirit.

The moment you realize you are judging, go within and choose again.

The moment you recognize you are listening to ego as your teacher, go within and choose again.

The moment you wake up to the truth that you have been asleep, go within and choose again.

You have the freedom to choose always!

Your heart is always ready to lead you. Your unique recipe for healing and vibrant health already exists in your heart. Your path to awakening and enlightenment is already programmed through your internal GPS. Your dreams have already come to fruition. Now you simply need to follow your heart and it will lead you directly to your dream and so much more than you can imagine. Follow the sign posts, trust your intuition, take inspired action, and surrender your life to Spirit.

Spirit is infinitely patient and always waiting for you to say YES to alignment. Your heart is always ready to lead you when you are willing to be led. Stop looking at "No" and be open to "YES!" Stop staring at the doors that are closed and go within for guidance. Spirit is likely directing you toward your next YES! Are you willing to follow the wisdom and loving voice that is leading you to everything you are meant to have and so much more? The life of your dreams is waiting for you to say, "YES!", so you can follow Spirit on the most direct route. No more ego detours. We are going for pure joy and happiness. Go within and choose again as often as you need to. Be kind to self, and love yourself unconditionally. I promise when you discover your YES for life, you will experience miracle, after miracle, after miracle.

> Go within and choose again as often as you need to.

The world is waiting for you to say, "YES!" Your soul is waiting for you to say, "YES!" So what do you say?

It is your time to choose.

Chapter 10

Heart Led Living Principle ~ Expect Miracles

A Course in Miracles defines a miracle as, "a shift from fear to love". In every moment, we make a choice to align with love or fear. My intention is to inspire you to make a conscious choice for love as often as you can. Whenever you choose love, you become open to experience a miracle. Some miracles are big and some are small, depending on the shift that occurs. Einstein wrote, "There are only two ways to live your life, one is as though nothing is a miracle, the other as though everything is a miracle." The choice is yours, but I promise you that if you start to see everything as a miracle, your life will expand in ways you could never begin to imagine.

I Remember JOY!

Joy is our natural state of being. We are designed to experience the deep pleasure of joy, yet so many people are detached from feeling joy. We have bought into the lie told by our ego that the world is out to get us and that in order to survive we need to protect ourselves from getting hurt. We are taught that pain and suffering are inevitable and normal.

If you align with ego and believe this lie, then pain and suffering will be your reality. After all, we create our own reality. Our thoughts fuel our emotions, our emotions send a vibration to the Universe, and the Universe responds. This is the foundation of the Law of Vibration and the secondary Law of Attraction. What you put out, you attract through vibrational resonance. Love and joy are powerful emotions with the highest vibrating calibration and frequency. Pain, fear, and suffering are the lowest.

| Joy is our natural state of being. |

When I first opened my mind-body studio, someone asked me what brought me joy? The very first words that popped into my mind were, "joy smoy". "Joy" was not a word I used in my vocabulary. It had been so long since I had experienced joy that it was completely foreign to me. I had been so deep in my pain and suffering for so long that I had no concept of joy.

I started to explore what joy meant to me: when did I last feel it? How did it feel? Where was it stored? How could I access it? Why was I so disconnected from it? Even when my son was born, I had felt happiness and gratitude, but I hadn't felt joy. I actually had to go back to childhood memories to remember the feeling of joy.

When my mentor Dr. Christiane Northrup shared her perspective around suffering and pleasure during one of our monthly team telegatherings, I had a huge and holy shift. For me suffering was pleasure. The two were intertwined; my ego was playing a clever game of pain and pleasure. Pain was comforting, because it was familiar. It was all I had known for so long that it had become my most reliable friend.

After that call, I decided that pain was not my boss nor was it my friend, and I made a conscious effort to allow joy back into my life. When I purposefully opened my heart and mind to joy I experienced a breakthrough. One morning during my yoga practice, I suddenly felt a wave of joy enter every cell of my body. My mind and my heart were united, and there was a beautiful light surrounding me. All fear and doubt dissolved instantly, and I was smiling on the inside and out. At first, it was overwhelming to the point where tears ran down my cheeks. Tears of joy!

Through the eyes of joy, I was able to receive my husband's love fully and completely. My heart was open and ready to receive love once again. I was no longer afraid to let joy in. At the time, my journey through fertility had closed my heart even more, and

I was so afraid to love fully. I thought a baby was the only thing that could possibly make me happy. I realized, however, that the only happiness I am ever going to find is the happiness I decide to create within. It is not out there somewhere; it is within me.

As I continue to open my heart to more and more joy each day, I begin to feel more alive inside. This is an area I am still very conscious and committed to. I have found inner peace, but deep inner joy is still my heart's work. I consciously invite it into my life.

> I have found inner peace, but deep inner joy is still my heart's work.

Are you willing to release your attachment to pain and suffering, and invite joy into your life once again? Are you willing to feel joy at the deepest level and remember it as your natural state? Imagine how much your life would change if you were experiencing joy on a daily basis. Joy, love, happiness, and gratitude are all high vibrating states of being. When you choose to feel joy, you choose to align with Spirit. When you align with Spirit and send the vibration of love and joy out to the Universe, you can expect miracles to be abundant.

♥ Heart Work: JOY List

Find a sacred space and begin to explore joy. Write a list of twenty things that bring you joy. You may need to go back into your childhood to reconnect to memories of joy. Write as many as you can the first time and continue to add onto the list until you have at least twenty. You can use this list when you feel you need a joy boost, by picking one thing on the list to do.

Here are twenty things on my current list that make my heart smile. I hope they will inspire you.

1. *Kisses from my horse.*
2. *Spending time with all the critters on my farm.*

3. *Boating with my family and being on the ocean.*
4. *Yoga and meditation.*
5. *Belly dancing.*
6. *When my little Chihuahua jumps up and down on her back legs like a leaping lemur.*
7. *When my son tells me it feels warm in his heart to snuggle with me.*
8. *Sitting under a huge umbrella-tree in a park near my home.*
9. *Inspiring others to say "YES!" to their health.*
10. *Leading my Heart Led Living community calls.*
11. *When my husband looks at me every morning with more love in his eyes than the day before.*
12. *Helping others see the invisible so they can heal at the deepest possible level.*
13. *Being home each night to have dinner with my family.*
14. *Growing fresh berries, vegetables, and fruit in my backyard.*
15. *Finding the moon in the sky every evening as I put my animals to bed.*
16. *Working from home and being there for my kids before and after school.*
17. *Having the freedom to follow my heart in my business.*
18. *Watching my stepdaughter be true to herself in spite of external pressures. Her courage inspires me every day!*
19. *Witnessing the miracles of healing with my clients and Heart Led Living members.*
20. *Speaking on stage to large audiences and sharing my heart's message.*

Miracles Turn It All Around

In *Heart Led Living*, we expect miracles. We are wide open to receive, witness and experience miracles in every moment. Miracles are available to everyone. In fact, miracles are occurring all the time with or without our awareness. Imagine if we all sat in awe of each and every miracle and took the time to celebrate each one.

When I was a child, I used to draw pictures of the house and property I wanted when I grew up. I would have a big house, with a barn full of animals, including horses and goats. When

I met my husband, he also wanted to live on a farm and have a horse. He wasn't so keen on having a goat, and he would laugh every time I brought it up, because I would get so giddy with excitement. We shared the same dream, but the money wasn't there to make it come to fruition. Yet, we continued living with the idea that one day we would have a farm.

In 2009, we were in the worst financial position, with about $300,000 in debt on top of our mortgage and my studio lease. The recession in 2008 had affected both our businesses, and we had to live off our line of credit to support them and our family. In the fall of 2009, I really wanted to start the adoption home study, which cost $3,500. Since we were reaching the end of our credit limit, it was hard to justify spending the money, but deep in my heart I just knew it was something we needed to do. So I spoke to my husband and asked for his support. He was concerned, because neither of our businesses were bringing in enough money to cover our expenses; we were still relying on a credit line to pay our monthly bills.

Miracle Number One:

Out of the blue, our new bank manager called to tell us that he was reviewing our file and realized he could increase our home line of credit if we needed it. We decided we could really use some more breathing room until our income increased, so we said, "Yes!" Now that there was a little bit more money to access, I asked my husband again about the $3,500. He was still concerned.

The words came flying out of my mouth before I could even think, "If I make $500,000 within the next six months, can I spend the money and start the home-study?" His answer was an immediate "Yes!" That helped, because I realized it wasn't about him doubting the adoption, he was simply worried about the money. Then I asked, "Can we start the home-study now and then I will make $500,000 within the next six months?" He said,

"Yes!"

We both felt, deep in our hearts, that $500,000 was possible, as long as we aligned fully with that vision. It was so clearly heart-led, and the amount resonated for both of us. So I spent the $3,500 from our line of credit and we started the home study. I set an intention to be wildly open to receive and be fully aligned with making $500,000. I received confirmation from everyone I spoke to. When I mentioned it to my mentor and coach, Les Brown, he said, "Yes, that would be easy to do." I felt such alignment with the belief that it was possible. I didn't know how, but I knew it was possible.

Miracle Number Two:

Three months had passed and suddenly I heard a knock at the door. It was a realtor who wanted to know if we were interested in selling our home. My first response was, "No." We had no intention of selling our home. He mentioned, before he left, that our home had gone up in value by $300,000 in the last three months. That same evening, my husband arrived home and told me a friend had just bought a house outside the city for $500,000. It was a newer and bigger home, with a large property. Remember, I was wide open to any signposts, so I saw what Spirit was showing me. I explained to my husband that if we sold our house and moved outside the city, we would be debt-free and mortgage-free. We agreed to meet with our realtor and gather more information.

Miracle Number Three:

Apparently, there was a huge demand for properties in our neigh-bourhood in Richmond, British Columbia, so the value of our house was double what we had thought and was now worth four times what we had paid for it. At the same time, the area just outside the city we were interested in was a buyer's market. We listed our home; it received two offers; it sold the first day.

Miracle Number Four:

We looked at many houses and, while the prices were right, we didn't find a house we loved right away. After looking for several weeks, we decided to make an offer on a house that we liked. The backyard was small, but the house was in a good neighborhood and had a lot of character. It turns out there was another offer that came in just before ours and we didn't get the house. My husband was discouraged and worried that we had made the wrong decision to sell our house. I knew his ego was coming in strongly, so I held my light and stayed in alignment with my heart, knowing that the perfect house was out there but we just hadn't come across it yet.

After a few days, my husband decided to change his mindset and open up his search criteria. He was very excited to show me one home he had found, but when I looked at the listing it was a 1400-square-foot two-bedroom rancher. Although it was on an acre of land and had a barn, the actual house was tiny. He pointed out that the unfinished basement made the house 2800-square-feet in total. We decided to take a look. Of all the houses we walked through, this one needed the most work. The moment I walked on to the back property, saw the fish-bearing stream, and crossed over the bridge to the barn, everything inside me jumped. "This is it! This is our property!" I knew we would need to invest in renovating the inside of the entire house, but we could afford to do that now.

Our shared dream of having a farm one day had fallen into our laps. Most of the properties of this size in the area were double what they were asking. We could now afford our dream home.

Miracle Number Five:

We were so excited to get the call to say they had accepted our offer. We had the farm we always wanted. I immediately started looking for a goat. Yes, I was all giddy! When I calculated all the expenses and income from selling our previous home, the profit before purchasing our new home was $497,000. Considering I had already spent the $3,500, we were right on the money with my intention of making $500,000 within six months. The month we moved was exactly six months from the date I set the intention.

This was a huge miracle that I continue to celebrate every time I look out my window and see my horse. I feel such gratitude every time I go outside to collect the eggs from my chickens and feed my critters. I am in awe of the five miracles that aligned us with our dream at a time when we thought it was impossible. Today, I don't believe in "impossible". When you are in alignment with your heart's path, anything is possible.

> I am in awe of the five miracles that aligned us with our dream at a time when we thought it was impossible. Today, I don't believe in "impossible".

♥ Heart Work: Celebrate the Miracles

Take a pen and paper, and find stillness. Close your eyes and take ten deep breaths. Imagine your mind wide open. Reflect back on the last week and start writing down all the miracles that occurred for you as well as the ones you witnessed for others. Write them all, big or small. Every miracle is a miracle to celebrate.

Once you have written down every miracle that came into your mind, invite the feeling of gratitude into your heart. Let it warm you from the inside as you bathe your mind in the miracle of celebration. For every miracle that arises from this moment on, take a moment to say, "Thank you."

The Miracle of Surrender

Just when we think we have it all figured out, along comes another brick wall. We can either get all bent out of shape and move into judgment about it, or we can remain curious and open to the guidance in each moment. Life is designed to awaken our soul. It is our response to life's challenges that will determine our experience. Life is happening for us, even when it shows up as pain, suffering, and sickness. The process of surrender is essential, especially when it comes to trying to make sense of everything showing up on our path.

Just when I was convinced that my health was improving and that I felt better than I ever had in my entire life, a cluster of health challenges showed up on my path. I was guided to see some local doctors and have some tests done. Most of the results came back "normal". but again I didn't feel "normal". At the end of November 2013, I found myself on the couch for two weeks, barely able to function. While I continued to take care of my family, animals, and did the minimum amount of work I could manage, I was exhausted and felt completely depleted. With only a few abnormal tests to cling to, my ego was desperate for answers. The fear of cancer crept in once more.

When I went into meditation, I was guided to go back to Sanoviv Medical Institute in Mexico. My immediate thought was, "Well, if I am meant to go back to Sanoviv, I will expect a miracle for the money showing up." Then I was shown to ask my paternal grandmother. Curiously, just a few weeks earlier I had been talking with her and she asked me if I needed any money. I had said, "No", but she insisted that if I ever needed money for anything that I should simply ask her.

Asking for help has become easier for me, but asking for money is still difficult. It became another powerful lesson in receiving. When I called her explaining I needed some money to go back to Sanoviv, without hesitation she asked, "How much money do you need?"

I had never asked her for money before. She was so happy to give me the money; in fact, I believe she had been waiting for me to ask for a long time. I felt the joy in her heart expand when she was able to give me this monetary gift.

When I arrived at Sanoviv Medical Institute, we began the

process of detoxification and testing right away. Within a few days, my doctor was stumped. He ruled out each theory with most tests coming back normal. I felt like a patient from the TV show *House* where all the doctors are left scratching their heads. During the first three days, I felt even worse and my doctor recommended bringing in an internal specialist. He wanted to make sure he wasn't missing something. I just wanted to know what was wrong with me. If they could just shine light on what it was, I knew I could heal it. I just couldn't get past the fear. On my first visit to Sanoviv, I knew I had cancer; this time, I was afraid I had cancer.

When the internal specialist arrived, he asked a few odd questions which led me to believe he hadn't read my chart. He asked about my symptoms and my history with drugs and alcohol and, immediately, I felt a shift in his energy. He moved into judgment and it felt familiar. My first thought was, "Here we go again." My second thought was, "Remain open."

He looked at me and said "Do you feel depressed?"

That was it; he had slapped a label on my forehead and decided I needed antidepressants. I went back to my room and I was furious. I started cursing, yelling, kicking my bed, and punching my pillows. I was like a toddler having a temper tantrum. A wave of deep rage was surfacing and there was no stopping the expression of it.

Memories of being hospitalized when I was around three-years-old flooded into my awareness. I was placed in a crib and left in a cold dark room all by myself. I was yelling for someone to come and help me, because I needed to go to the bathroom. No one came. I ended up soiling my sheets. I remember feeling so embarrassed, until suddenly an anger washed over me as I picked up my feces and started throwing it and smearing it all over the crib. I have had vague memories of that childhood trauma before, but this was the first time I had got in touch with the deep anger I had felt. Still no one came. Exhausted, defeated, and all alone, I curled up in a ball on my soiled bed and cried myself to sleep.

Curled up in a ball on my bed at Sanoviv, I re-lived that memory and allowed space for all the anger and shame to surface. I realized where my distrust in the medical system came from. I felt a shift from anger to confusion. I reached out for support and called my husband back home. I was wide open and willing to see the truth. I asked him if I was missing something and whether he thought I was depressed.

He said, "No. I know the symptoms of depression and you do not have any of those symptoms."

I reached out to Lisa and asked her the same question. I was willing to heal. I was open to anything and attached to nothing. Lisa actually laughed at the doctor's conclusion and said, "People who are depressed don't do the work you do in this world. Your work is complete."

That night I surrendered everything and I mean **everything.** I broke down and completely surrendered my need to know. I made peace with the idea that I may feel sick for the rest of my life. If that is my path then so be it. I declared that even if my body continues to feel like crap, no one could take away the joy in my heart. I surrendered the need to fix or heal my own body. As an intuitive healer, I felt pressure to heal myself. I gave Spirit all my research, all my symptoms, questions, concerns, results, doctors, and everything else.

> I declared that even if my body continues to feel like crap, no one could take away the joy in my heart. I surrendered the need to fix or heal my own body.

Lisa's words, "Your work is complete," landed directly into my heart. A huge pressure of responsibility was lifted from my mind and body. I realized that whether I die today or in ten years, my heart work is complete. There is nothing else to do in this moment, other than to surrender to what is.

As I lay there looking directly at my own death, I felt no fear. Instead, I felt a deep sense of relief and a blanket of pure love. I connected to a deep trust within my heart that everything is playing out the way it is meant to play out and it is only from my human perspective that I can't explain it. In the eyes of Spirit, all is well and all will be well.

As I let go and completely surrendered, I freed my doctor from finding a diagnosis. I no longer felt the need to know what was wrong with me. Nothing was wrong; in fact, everything was perfect. I directed Spirit that if there was anything I needed to know, to let it come with ease and grace; otherwise I let go and trust my path. The joy in my heart expanded, and although my body still felt heavy, my heart and mind were lighter. The anger had left my body and I felt nothing but gratitude toward the specialist, because he had helped me get to the deep anger I was holding in my pelvis all these years. He was an angel in disguise shining light on the childhood wound that needed to be healed. Gratitude filled my heart and I was at peace once again.

The next morning, I met with my original doctor from Sanoviv and explained the miracle I had experienced. He was excited for the shift and healing that had occurred emotionally, but he was even more excited because he had a diagnosis for me. As he was driving, the diagnosis suddenly popped into his mind like a download. He was so excited that he had to pull over to the side of the road to look it up on the internet. It was a form of vitamin toxicity that wasn't very common, but—because my liver was compromised—over time it had accumulated in my body until it reached toxic levels. As he listed all the symptoms, everything clicked and even symptoms I had dismissed as unrelated, suddenly fitted. It was another miracle. We started right away on a treatment plan and IV therapy, and the next morning I felt so much better.

When I surrendered my need to know, which was my ego convincing me I had to heal, I created space for peace and I was able to return to alignment even though my symptoms were still present. The miracles came and continue to come. I am feeling stronger than ever in my mind and I know this process of unwinding and healing my body is part of my path.

When we surrender fully and choose alignment with Spirit over everything else, we shift into a place of trust. We need to be willing to let go of everything we think we know and everything we think we don't know. In doing so, we align with the path that is meant for our highest good.

When you practise heart-led living in every area of your life, you will experience miracles frequently, because they are the side effects of alignment. There are no coincidences, only divine timing and miraculous alignment. Align with Spirit, lead with your heart, follow the signposts, take inspired action when guided, hold your light with certainty, and I promise you that miracles will be abundant. As Einstein suggests, live your life as if everything is a miracle. If everything is a miracle that means that YOU are a miracle too!

Epilogue

Creating a Foundation for Your Heart-Led Life

I am so grateful you have embarked on this journey with me. Now it is your turn to discover your most direct path to living a heart-led life. I have shared some foundational tools, wisdom and principles of *Heart Led Living* and now it is your turn to integrate them into every area of your life. The best place to begin is here and now. Let the words in this book meet you where you are without judgment. Everyone's path is unique.

Find stillness, take a deep breath, and set an intention to let your heart take the lead. Not all the tools will be appropriate for you at this time. Some tools you may never be guided to use. Take the ones that resonate deep within your heart and let the others go for now. When you follow your heart and let Spirit lead you in each and every moment, you will tap into a divine energy that will carry you through all life's challenges.

Remember: life is designed to awaken your soul; everything that is on your path has purpose. As you begin to unwind from everything you think you know, remain open to anything and at the same time, be attached to nothing. This will be extremely helpful in the process of unwinding. Eventually some of the tools you are using daily will no longer work or resonate. This is when you will make a conscious choice to allow them to drop away. Once they have served their purpose, you need to let them go. Trust your intuition. Often you will feel resistance deep inside before you have a mental awareness of it.

> Remember: life is designed to awaken your soul; everything that is on your path has purpose.

I designed this book to be an introduction to the *Heart Led Living* principles. As you continue to deeply unwind and align with Spirit, eventually you may be able to let go of this book all together. Perhaps you will be guided to gift it to someone else or leave it on a table at a coffee shop or donate it to a local community centre. Once you have fully integrated these ten *Heart Led Living* principles, you no longer need this book. This is good news, because that is when you can delve deeper into heart-led living.

The deeper work comes after the integration of the ten principles. Even for me. After writing this book, I have been able to fully integrate these principles and now I am guided to release them with love. This will happen to you in your own time. Trust the process of unwinding and integration.

There will come a time when you have to let go of everything I have taught you here. You will be asked to surrender everything you think you know, in order to align with the deeper truth. If you need support during this time, come visit my website at www. heartledliving.com. You may be inspired to join our community so that you can learn how to deepen into your soul's truth.

It is an exciting time of awakening and, while there is a quickening, we also need to respect our own path and divine timing. Some of you will be ready to hear this next piece and for others I am simply planting a seed that may or may not resonate at this time; here goes.

The Truth is you are already healed. You are not broken and you don't need to be fixed. In fact, you are perfect love, because you come from perfect love. You only need these tools, because you believe you need them. You only need healing, because you believe you need healing. In the eyes of Spirit, you are already healed. You are light. You are love. You are one with Spirit. There is no separation except the thought in your mind that you are separate.

> You are perfect love, because you come from perfect love.

Here are the ten principles again.

Be willing to heal
Choose love
Hold your light
Take inspired action only
Fill your heart first
Be open to anything
Be curious
Be attached to nothing
Lead with your heart
Expect miracles

Take the ones that resonate and use them for as long as they resonate. Then be willing to let it go and trust your heart as it leads you with each breath.

You are exactly where you need to be, doing exactly what you need to be doing. Everything up until this moment has been purposeful and as you continue to follow your heart, you will be guided in each moment.

Author Biography

Sue Dumais is a *Heart Led Living* Coach, an Author, an International Speaker, and a gifted Intuitive Healer who helps others see the invisible, feel the intangible, and do the impossible. She brings the gift of insight, awareness, and self-empowerment to her audiences. She is passionate about helping others heal the root of their dis-eases and return physically, mentally, emotionally, spiritually, and energetically to their natural state of harmony.

Desperately seeking answers for herself, Sue Dumais has walked to the edge of life over and over again, asking "Why am I here?" At a deep level, she believed she wasn't good enough, even while she was constantly striving to prove her own worth. After sensing cancer deep within her own body, Sue discovered her unique healing path back to vibrant health. Her deep desire to understand human behaviour and to heal her past has led her to become a coach and embrace her intuitive gifts as a healer. www.HeartLedLiving.com

Sue's new book *Heart Led Living ~ When Hard Work Becomes Heart Work* describes her personal journey through the darkness of anorexia, alcohol abuse, and other self-destructive behaviours. En route, she discovers her true gift of inspiring others to awaken their innate ability to heal and to trust their intuition as they lead with their heart and discover their "YES!" for life.

Online Program and Resources

Fertility Yoga & Meditation Kit (www.familypassages.ca)
Fertility Yoga downloadable classes (www.familypassages.ca)
Protecting Your Precious Energy audio program (www.heartledliving.com)
Heart Led Living Community (www.heartledliving.com)
Heart Centered Speaker Training (www.heartledliving.com/speaker-training)
Expect Miracles! Online Radio Show (www.intentionradio.com)

Online Courses for Fitness and Yoga Instructors

Fertility Yoga Teacher Training
Fitness Fertility Specialist Certification
Pre & Post Natal Fitness Certification
and other BCRPA/AFLCA/CMT approved online courses:
www.familypassages.ca

Other Books

Yoga for Fertility Handbook
A Strong Core for Life

Intuitive Healing Sessions

For more information on booking a private session/reading with Sue Dumais, visit www.heartledliving.com/intuitivehealing

Hire Sue Dumais as a speaker

Sue Dumais has shared the stage with **Dr Christiane Northrup, Dr Dennis Waitely, Marianne Williamson** and **Les Brown**. She truly owns her power on stage and has been teaching, speaking, and training for more than 20 years. Sue has been trained and mentored by Les Brown, one of the top 5 speakers in the world, and she has spoken in front of audiences 10,000 strong with unshakeable confidence. To hire Sue as a speaker visit www.thefertilityeffect.com

Websites

Heart Led Living: www.heartledliving.com
Family Passages: www.familypassages.ca
The Fertility Effect: www.thefertilityeffect.com

Social Media

Face Book:
www.facebook.com/heartledliving
www.facebook.com/pages/Sue-Dumais/173089822758366

Twitter: witter.com/heartledliving
twitter.com/fertilityyoga
LinkedIn Page: www.linkedin.com/pub/sue-dumais/1/123/85

Blog Page: heartledliving.com/blog/
Pinterest Page: pinterest.com/suedumais/boards/
YouTube Account: www.youtube.com/user/SueDumais

If you want to get on the path to be a published author with Life Journey Publishing (a division of Influence Publishing), please go to
www.InfluencePublishing.com/InspireABook

Inspiring books that influence change

More information on our other titles and how to submit your own proposal can be found at
www.InfluencePublishing.com